Hanna's Diary, 1938–1941

Hanna's Diary, 1938–1941

Czechoslovakia to Canada

HANNA SPENCER

McGill-Queen's University Press

Montreal & Kingston · London · Ithaca

© McGill-Queen's University Press 2001
ISBN 0-7735-2231-x
Legal deposit third quarter 2001
Bibliothèque nationale du Québec

Printed in Canada on acid-free paper
Reprinted 2002

McGill-Queen's University Press acknowledges the financial support of the Government of Canada through the Book Publishing Industry Development ment Program (BPIDP) for its activities. It also acknowledges the support of the Canada Council for the Arts for its publishing program.

Canadian Cataloguing in Publication Data

Spencer, Hanna
    Hanna's diary, 1938–1941: Czechoslovakia to Canada
    Includes index.
    ISBN 0-7735-2231-x
    1. Spencer, Hanna – Diaries. 2. Refugees, Jewish – Czechoslovakia – Diaries. 3. Refugees, Jewish – Canada – Diaries. 4. World War, 1939–1945 – Refugees – Biography. 5. Czech Canadians – Biography. I. Title

D811.5.S67 2001   940.53'089'9240437   C00-901670-8

This book was typeset by Dynagram Inc. in 11/13.5 Caslon.

To our children Erica and Martin and our grandchildren Hilary, Gregory, Nicole, Laura, and Justine

Contents

Illustrations

Preface

For forty-five years I had not opened the wooden box with the fancy hand-carved lid. I knew what was in it. Together with miscellaneous keepsakes and photographs, it contained six notebooks written in German. This was the journal that I kept from 1938 to 1941, during a crucial period in many people's lives, including mine. The box had remained locked since 1942, when I had pulled down my own "iron curtain," shutting out the memories preserved on those pages. But the time eventually came for the curtain to be raised. The main reason for this change of mind was my profound regret that I had not quizzed my parents more about their personal history; I didn't want this to happen to my children and grandchildren. Thus I brought myself to open the box, literally and figuratively, and set about translating the diaries from German into English – strictly for the use of my family, or so I thought.

Now another and even bigger hurdle is being passed in allowing these diaries to be made public. The credit for this – or should I say blame? – is due entirely to those friends and family members who persuaded me that my story would be of interest to readers beyond the circle of family and friends. Among the encouraging voices, the most compelling and persistent was that of Carlotta Lemieux, and I cannot thank her enough. Having encouraged and prodded me to undertake this project in the first place, Carlotta advised and guided me, generously allowing me to benefit from her experience as editor par excellence. I am grateful to my family, who cheered me on, but above all I thank my husband Elvins, who has been a loving, supportive partner for fifty-eight years (and counting) and without whose understanding and support this manuscript would not have seen the light of day.

Hanna Spencer
London, Ontario
November 2000

Introduction

This diary was begun in 1938, when Hitler's shadow was spreading ever more ominously across Europe. He had already annexed Austria, and Czechoslovakia seemed next on his list of targets. This was a matter of particular anxiety to Jewish families such as mine.

Czechoslovakia was still a very young country, one of the new democracies created in 1918 at the end of World War I. Long known as Bohemia, Moravia, Silesia, and Slovakia, the area had been part of the Austro-Hungarian Empire for centuries, and I was in fact born in Austria. I was four years old when the new state was founded.

The Czechs had hopes of building a model republic under their revered philosopher president, Thomas G. Masaryk, but there were problems from the start. Czechoslovakia had inherited a sizable population of Sudeten Germans, who lived mainly in the mountains along the border with Germany and Austria. Under the empire, their language and culture had been dominant – for centuries they had been the masters – and they resented their minority position within the Czechoslovak state. The situation was aggravated by the Great Depression of the 1930s, which was felt more painfully in the industrialized Sudeten than in the more agricultural Czech areas. But above all, Hitler had come to power in Germany in 1933, and as his influence and domination escalated, so did the demands of the Sudeten Germans. Led by Konrad Henlein, who in fact took his marching orders from Hitler, they became increasingly vocal and finally demanded to be united with the German Reich.

At that time, my family was living in Komotau,[1] in the German-speaking part of western Bohemia. It was there I attended high school and it was there I met Hans Feiertag, for whom my diary was written. Hans was two years ahead of me at school – a tall, blond Austrian boy; a Christian. I had noticed him during recess, and I soon became aware that he had noticed me too. Then came the time when all the girls in my class were looking forward to *Tanzstunde,* the course in ballroom dancing, sponsored by the school. Girls of the Sexta were to be partnered by the boys of the Octava (grades 11 and 13, respectively). Convention demanded that in order to attend, each girl had to be personally and formally invited by a partner who thereby became her *Haupttänzer,* her principal partner. I was worried. Who would want to partner the Jewish girl? My good friend Erich Heller[2] was the only Jewish student in the Octava, but he had already made clear that he was not interested in such bourgeois rituals. It was with relief as much as delight that I received a visit at home from a very nervous Hans, who had come to invite me to be his dancing partner.

Of course, everyone in Komotau knew that the Fischl family was Jewish, though we were completely assimilated, as were most Jews in Czechoslovakia. I didn't feel particularly Jewish. We did not observe the Sabbath or any dietary laws, and we went to the synagogue only once a year, on Yom Kippur, the Day of Atonement. Growing up in a predominantly Christian community, my younger sister Mimi and I were more familiar with Catholic than Jewish traditions. We looked forward to St Niklas Day and Christmas as the big events of the year, complete with our own Christmas tree.

We were not a wealthy family. "Average middle class" would probably describe us best. One of the few members of the family who could be considered wealthy was my father's younger brother, my beloved Uncle Louis, a born entrepreneur who owned a glove-making factory in Bärringen, near Karlsbad, and seemed to have travelled all over the world. By contrast, my father's business interests were modest.

It was always assumed that I would go to university. So in 1932 I enrolled at the German University in Prague to study Germanic and

Slavonic languages and literatures. Hans, meanwhile, was studying at
the Musik Akademie in Vienna. His absorbing interest in music had
emerged early on. When I first met him, he was already an accomplished pianist and viola player, and music obviously was more to him
than a hobby.

Our dancing partnership turned into a friendship that continued
after *Tanzstunde* and after Hans left for Vienna. While apart, we corresponded almost daily, and during vacations he was a regular visitor
in our home, beloved by the whole family. We spent much time ex-
ploring the countryside, making music, and reading together. During
my student days in Prague, Hans transferred there for some semesters;
and later, after I obtained my PH D and had begun life as a teacher in
Olmütz, we often met in Vienna, which was only a few hours away by
train.

Olmütz was a middle-sized town on the border between the
Czech- and German-speaking parts of Moravia. The population
there was predominantly German, though of course language presented me with no problems, since German and Czech were my specialty. In any case, Mimi and I had been brought up to speak both
languages.

Vienna was a magical city, and Hans and I revelled in its delights. But
while we were attending concerts together or enjoying hiking excursions
in the Alps, we were aware of the darkening clouds over Europe. Hitler
had taken over as German chancellor around the time I was first settling
in as a student in Prague, and since then he had been increasingly assert-
ing his power, step by step, and had unilaterally cancelled the conditions
which the Treaty of Versailles had imposed on Germany after World
War I. He had created a standing army, occupied the Rhineland, and introduced the notorious Nuremberg Laws, which deprived Jews of their
civil rights, took away their possessions, denied them access to educa-
tional and cultural facilities of any kind, stripped them of their academic
degrees, and reduced them to a subhuman status. Edict after oppressive
edict gradually turned Jews into pariahs, finally prohibiting contact with
them altogether.[3]

The Feiertags, Hans's family, were natives of Vienna and had remained Austrian citizens. When in March 1938 Hitler's army marched into Austria, declaring it to be an integral part of Germany, we knew that disaster had struck. Hans was now a German citizen. Clearly, he and I could no longer be seen to be associated with each other in any way. Hans had begun to establish himself as a promising young composer – already his works were being played in concerts and on the radio. If his relationship with a Jew became known, it would end his musical career and make him an outcast too.

It was then that he suggested I write a diary so that he might catch up with me (or so he put it) when we could be together again. We hoped this would be just a matter of "when." It is this diary that fills the following pages. Six of the seven notebooks were originally written in German, and I translated them to make them available to my family. Only later did friends suggest that others also might find them of interest.[4]

Unlike most diaries, this is not a monologue; it is a one-sided dialogue. Most of the time I am addressing Hans Feiertag, or at least speaking for his benefit; for we not only avoided being seen together but were afraid to correspond directly. We resorted to using third parties as intermediaries, especially my friend Hella Popp, and this naturally limited the frequency of our letters. So instead of sharing our thoughts and feelings on an almost daily basis as we had been doing for eight years, we could only send signs of life – desperate greetings to show that we were still in each other's mind, and hoping. The diary would give us a chance to fill in the gap, as it were, later on. Somehow we still clung to the hope that there would be a joint "later on." For me, this belief had almost become an existential necessity. For eight years, I had merged and subordinated my life, my thoughts, my wishes to his. Without Hans, my life seemed empty, without purpose.

How had Hans achieved such a powerful, indeed overpowering, hold on me? He seemed above all concerned to help me develop and grow and be creative, yet our joint aspirations centred on him and his work. He was a very special person, different from anyone I have ever known;

utterly uninterested in trivia or what he took for trivia – mere external, superficial matters, in which he even included concern with creature comforts at the expense of spiritual values. I was captivated by his vision, his intensity, his mystique. He was creative and talented in many ways; he could draw, he could carve figures out of wood and bark, but first and foremost came his commitment to music. And being involved with him, loving him, I became infected and affected by his sense of the importance of his work. He seemed to have no choice. His dedication to composing was all-consuming: he had not merely chosen music as his career; it was as if music had chosen him. It was a mission in which he rejoiced, and at times a burden from which he suffered. Even watching him play the piano, his facial muscles twitching and pulling with every note, made one realize that he experienced music differently from the way we ordinary mortals do.

This little profile of Hans Feiertag may help explain the purpose and focus of this journal, and why it was so important for me to disappear from his life – or rather, to appear to have done so – at a time when the Nazis in Germany had come to power and their followers in the German areas of Czechoslovakia were gaining the upper hand. And why I never questioned or resented it. Hans Feiertag's musical progress, his acceptance by an audience, and the possibility of being performed and heard were more to him than a mere career or ambition; as well, his compositions – mostly songs or choral works – were intrinsically tied to the German language and, he felt, to a German audience. Thus I went along with the plan to "go underground," in the hope that the arrangement would be temporary. It was a hope that became increasingly difficult to maintain.

The journal begins in August 1938 during the last days of my summer vacation before I returned to my teaching job in Olmütz, where I had taught during the previous year. I was spending a few days with my Uncle Louis and Aunt Maña in Bärringen, near Karlsbad.

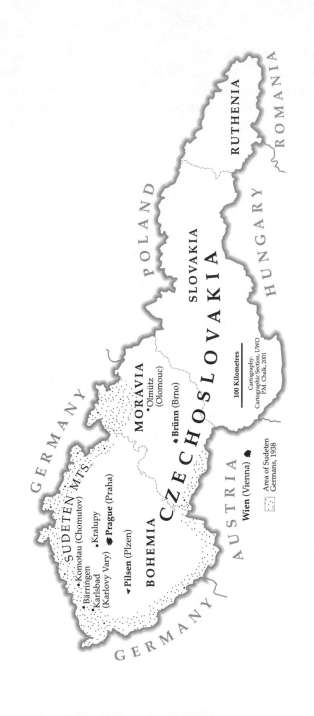

POLAND

ROMANIA

RUTHENIA

GERMANY

SLOVAKIA

HUNGARY

CZECHOSLOVAKIA

MORAVIA

Olmütz
(Olomouc)

Brünn (Brno)

SUDETEN MTS.

Komotau (Chomutov)

Kralupy

Prague (Praha)

Bärringen

Karlsbad
(Karlovy Vary)

Pilsen (Plzen)

BOHEMIA

AUSTRIA

Wien (Vienna)

GERMANY

100 Kilometres

Cartography:
Cartographic Section, UWO
P.M. Chalk, 2001

Area of Sudeten
Germans, 1938

Hanna's Diary, 1938–1941

I

Czechoslovakia

6 August – 24 October 1938

BÄRRINGEN, SATURDAY NOON, 6 AUGUST 1938
I have been here for two days. Nice that no one takes any notice of me all day, except three-year-old little Johnnie,[1] who is very sweet. I have spent the days sitting either in the garden or on a bench in the nearby forest, trying to read English, but can't seem to find the peace within me to settle down to it. The threat of war makes me anxious. And I don't know where H is. He wrote only that he is going away for a few days and that I could go away too until around 21 August. I have such a gorgeous tan – too bad that you can't see me. I think you are in Germany.[2]

MONDAY, 8 AUGUST
This has been a full day. I was sitting up in the woods, or rather at the edge, looking out on the wide panorama below me and listening to the mysterious rustle of the wind. It has been a truly summery day, the grass alive with humming and buzzing and scurrying creatures.

In the afternoon I rode out on my bike. A radiant afternoon. The landscape is incredibly pleasant. A motorcyclist passed me, and from behind he looked like H. I would like to sit with you in the forest and listen – in this friendly forest where every sound doesn't make one jump, scared to death.

I am reading an English mystery novel.

THURSDAY, 11 AUGUST
I am once again sitting on my favourite bench at the edge of the woods. Mountains, forest, roads, meadows, villages stretch out below,

as far as the horizon. A thought has just occurred to me. Although man seems to be the all-powerful master of the earth − more so than any other creature − is he really? At times he can be helpless like a flower or a stone. It seems to me that he has this earth on loan, just like an ant colony "owns" a piece of forest soil − until a stronger force destroys it. Sometimes we poke an anthill with a stick − a senseless act. Are the forces that dispose of us equally senseless? Or is there a meaning in it all?

Again no mail today. I wonder where you are. What can I give you for your birthday?

Someone just sat down on the bench beside me. Goodbye for now.

SATURDAY, 13 AUGUST

Just returned from a walk through the forest. It is a dull day with clouds, thick and heavy, hanging deep into the valley. The trees were standing completely silent, without even the slightest rustle.

I have been reading *Britta* by Bruno Brehm.[3] Had never read anything by him. Thank you for suggesting it.

The Fischls had an English guest yesterday. After supper, Maña[4] remarked that I speak English rather nicely, said she was surprised how much I knew. Today she said, out of the blue, "Hanni still hasn't lost her look of a wondering child." Needless to say, I had not been wondering about anything at the time, at least not until she said that. What I look like is very important to me now, more than ever before. Because the present doesn't count, I have to remain young as long as possible ...

Had a queasy stomach the last two days but am feeling better. For a while I felt so miserable that I thought this must be what it's like to be dying!

The folding chair on which I was sitting collapsed and dumped me into the lilacs. The blue mark on my arm looks most impressive − almost like some of the high-priced paintings in the Manes.[5] I am returning home tomorrow.

KOMOTAU, TUESDAY, 16 AUGUST

My first day home and immediately a wonderful encounter on the street![6] My heart pounded so, I thought it would jump out of my throat. H looks rather well; and the fact that he was already up at half-past nine is a good sign.

Now I can enjoy working again. Have also begun to brush up my French and shall be reading English and French books in turn. As well, I want to start preparing for school[7] but I'll leave that to the last. Cooked with Mutti[8] and then washed the dishes. Today ev-

Hanna Fischl, age twenty-four

erything gives me pleasure. I want to do good turns for everybody, and, above all, I feel like working *so* hard! Greetings, my dear, dear diary.[9]

WEDNESDAY, 17 AUGUST

There was a thunderstorm at 4:30 this afternoon. I went to town immediately afterwards but didn't meet H. In the morning, I rode out on the bike and looked at all our familiar spots. Sat for a long time under the big tree near Pirken, looking in all directions, and then I looked towards the two black towers near the house in which someone was perhaps playing the piano or sitting at the table near the window. My thoughts wandered back and forth over many years until they came to a silent moment in the forest. Your head was resting in my lap and we were alone in the world, you and I, very far from everything. I shall always remember what I secretly promised myself while you slept. And then we had to set each other free – you to work, me to prepare and wait. Which I have been doing.

FRIDAY, 19 AUGUST

Hooray! A letter from Olmütz that I have been promoted! From sessional to *provisorisch*.[10] I am delighted, really delighted.

On the last day in Bärringen, Maňa, Mimi,[11] and I had gone for a walk looking for mushrooms. Found nothing, of course. I prayed, "Please, please let us find one. If we do, I'll take it as a good omen for next year." Almost at once Maňa found a huge *Birkenpilz* right by the wayside.

Now I am going to wash my hair to look beautiful this afternoon. And lie in the sun for a bit. I think that something is in store for me during the next few days. Tomorrow is the twentieth, Papa's birthday. And the day after ...

Am reading a German book for a change: Franz Karl Ginzkey's *Der von der Vogelweide*, a biography of Walther.[12] Quite sentimental, and many contrived so-called rhymes. Quite a contrast to the last book I read, *La femme et le pantin*, very sensual and erotic. I prefer the Ginzkey.[13]

KOMOTAU, SUNDAY, 21 AUGUST

I am trying to hold onto last night's dream:[14]

First the ride, on a sweltering afternoon, in the hot, dusty train, winding its way through western Bohemia. I have an overwhelming desire to give in to tiredness or daydreams, and it takes an effort to stay alert so that I don't miss the short stop in J.[15]

A bench near the station. Waiting for the next train while darkness is falling. It is cooler now. Occasionally the distant sky is ripped open by lightning. Rumbling thunder far away. Another half-hour to wait. Will he come?

The train pulls in, almost passes the station before coming to a halt. A figure, barely visible, who had stood by the door of the coach, has emerged from the station and is now a silhouette, quite near. The other figure detaches itself from the bench. Without a word they move on together, enveloped in darkness. Just as they touch with a soft, hungry kiss, there is a brilliant flash in the sky. "Couldn't the lightning have waited?" On they walk, along the road that leads into the forest, a sleeping, silent forest; arm in arm, as if each is carried by the other. Talking, describing, chatting, asking, answering – so much to catch up on – all in a whisper. And in between, stop and listen. The arm around my shoulder feels soft and warm and comforting.

Then we turn off the path and enter the wood. We listen, we feel our way in the darkness, hand in hand. We find a spot. It is pitch-dark except for flashes of lightning now and then. We cling to each other as if for the last time. The forest around us stands completely silent. All creatures asleep except us. For you and me, this time is too precious for sleep.

The air is still warm. Ominously, the distant rumbling seems to come closer. All of a sudden there is a rush of wind in the treetops, first from one side, then the other, ever stronger, and now sounding above us like the roar of an ocean.

"Hans, this is scary."

"If you are scared, we'll go. But there's no hurry. In the meantime, be sure to remember everything: knapsack, jacket, flashlight ..."

"I've got mine. Have you?"

"Let's go."

We are back on the road. "Let's go faster."

"Don't be afraid. We are only a few minutes from the village." There! – a flash – and another. It is eerily beautiful. Open landscape now, momentarily bathed in blue light, ghostlike, then plunged once more into black utter darkness. A new burst of light, brilliant enough to make you feel that you are looking at the edge of the world. We shudder. The arm around me holds me very, very tightly.

"Isn't it marvellous?"

There, a drop. Bigger drops.

"Let's run."

But it is too late. It is as if the clouds are about to burst. Nowhere to hide, nowhere to run. At this very moment, sounds of an approaching car behind us – the sound we have been dreading all night. We hardly see the headlights. I hold out my hand, and it stops. It's a truck. Quickly, climb in. There are four of us in the two seats of the cabin. Impossible to drive on. The sky seems to have opened up.

The flashes of lightning are now followed immediately by crashing thunder. The woman between me and the driver is so scared she yells at her husband. Hansl sits on my lap, quietly, pressing my hand. With my other, I have to hold the door shut. What luck! What if the truck had not come just then on this lonely open road? We would have been drenched to the skin, at midnight, without a chance to dry out. Aren't we in luck after all!

Ten minutes later we drive into the village. Inside a house. The woman in her nightie, a naked little boy, two dogs. There we sit at the table, waiting for the storm to stop. A whole hour. Finally, at a quarter past one, the rain has almost stopped and we trudge on. We don't feel the dampness or the chill but tramp along happily. We stop for a kiss.

"Have you noticed that the rain has stopped?"

"What if war breaks out?"

"They'll shoot me." The sad quiver around your lips pierces me as much as your words. "Nothing gives me joy any more, Hanni. Without you, I have no inner peace. I can't work."

"But you know I belong to you more than ever — even if we aren't together."

"I know. But I have never needed you more." And then: "If only I could cope better. I have lost belief in myself." Again the quivering lips.

"If only I could help …"

"Do this for me. Write me a radio play about Walther von der Vogelweide, tying the songs together."

I promise to try.

"Not just try. You must do it. You know that all my *Vogelweide Lieder* are yours. Always will be."

I promise.

We walk on. A cyclist passes. On we walk, stopping from time to time, perhaps leaning against a tree. Roosters are beginning to crow and to answer one another. How much longer? Three more hours. Hold me tight, please. Leaning against a white stone marker by the side of the road, we wait for the day and wish it would never come. It is getting cool, and Hans puts on the new pullover I made him.

"A little wide across the shoulders — shall I fix it?"

"No. I'll grow into it."

"How about some pictures of yourself, Hannerl?" I promise, and you add: "Your eyes look the same as on the day I unexpectedly came home from Vienna – remember? The time I brought you the balloon. You literally jumped with joy."

We return to the station. Drink at the pump and wash. Suddenly panic. We have only fifteen minutes left. Buy tickets. The clerk is either stupid or half asleep – takes ages to find them, and the precious seconds tick away. Then in comes the train, and he is gone. I have to wait another hour and a half. Try to read the book he left me. But I am too weary and put my head on my arms. At last my train arrives. I have a seat up front, but I can't keep my eyes open.

And so I have slept on and dreamed. It is raining. They all have left the house. Everybody is gone. Everybody. So far, far away. I feel a little sick. But it's probably just tiredness. My thoughts can't let go of yesterday. It was the longest night of my life.

You told me some good news: you had a checkup and the X-ray showed that you are all right, no kidney stones. That's great news. And I am imagining how your folk, without an inkling of what you have been up to, suggest a little nap after lunch because you look tired, and how you keep on sleeping till nightfall.

One more thing: I shall remember one light-hearted moment. It was your laughter when I said, "If I am ever caught in the rain again, I'll tell myself, '*This* is *nothing!*'" Your laugh was so happy, almost carefree.

MONDAY, 22 AUGUST

Stayed in my room all yesterday afternoon. Only in the evening, when the others returned, did I go downstairs. The Priesen folk were here; lots of laughter with the Pollaks as always.[16]

I am happy to have a task: I am going to tackle the Walther play right away. It is to provide a framework for his songs. If it works, it may be a way to help H restore his confidence. Finished the Ginzkey book and started the other one.

Washed gloves, stockings, and a pullover, and after lunch, when I was too lazy to think, I wrote postcards to Erna and Helmar Frank, the school, Frau Kassal, and Traudl Holub, and a little letter to Herta Weiss,[17] as promised. Now back to real work. Thinking of you I feel both pain and pleasure. At least I know that for the moment you are well and safe.

TUESDAY, 23 AUGUST

I read Walther in the morning. In the afternoon, saw H accidentally, but only in the distance. As I passed the fruit stalls in the market, I saw him coming slowly from the direction of the school. I continued on my way. Perhaps I could have turned round and actually passed him. Why didn't I? He wore his new pullover.

No mail. Finished reading the book on Walther. Now I have to take pen in hand and begin. I have so little imagination! But it simply must work eventually if I persist. I am so glad H gave me a job to do. Perhaps I should have done the same to help him over his brooding stage. But he is different from me. He resists being made to do things, is more internally motivated. In any case, I couldn't think of a task to give him.

Around 4:30 PM[18] I wanted to walk the usual route but was intercepted by Pöschl[19] and couldn't get rid of him. He asked me to go out with him some evening. The only answer that came to mind was "I go to bed early." But what is one to say? Simply saying "No thank-you" sounds even worse – or does it?

A week from today is the first day of school. Then I won't be able to walk through the streets with pounding heart to see if a certain blond head pops up somewhere. I should have turned round yesterday for one last look into his eyes! If only he could relax and were able to work.

THURSDAY, 25 AUGUST

A letter with his photograph. This is the best present he could have given me. Those dear, deep eyes. The serious mouth, yet not hard. The chin somewhat more energetic, not childlike as before. And that mass of hair! But the hint of sadness around his mouth tears me apart. When will you be able to laugh again, freely and heartily, Sir Walther?

Tried to see him in the afternoon. No luck. Had a letter from Hella.[20] Poor thing, still struggling with her thesis. I answered right away. Tried to write the first scene of the play. We read so much nonsense – why couldn't I produce some too?

I am lying in bed now. Your picture is before me, two faithful eyes watching me as I write. And as they will every day. Good night.

Hans Feiertag, age twenty-five

FRIDAY, 26 AUGUST

Have been looking at your picture for a long time, so long that I almost forgot that it is only a photograph.

The political tension is worsening. I believe that no one wants war, but what sort of solution is there? Three letters today: Frau Kassal writes that I can have my room again but that the rent will be twenty crowns more. Helmar Frank writes, in English, mostly about Erna. I wonder what their relationship is. He is her student, and she says they are "only" friends; but I think they love each other. They made a trip to Italy together, sleeping in one tent. The third letter was from Herta Weiss.

Good night! I shall pray that all goes well. But how can it? I never understood you better than I do now. But never was there a greater abyss between us. Will it ever be bridged? Dear diary, I must not think, for there is no rational solution. I can only hope and have faith.

Rereading some of your letters helps. Here is one of them: "Getting a glimpse of you today was beautiful. I almost collided with another bicyclist – perhaps you noticed. You are nicely tanned but a little thin. Your eyes, so unspeakably dear, but looking a little sad, as if you had cried. A whole hour afterwards I felt almost as in a dream." And: "My dear, dear Hanni, don't be sad. We belong together, you and I. I have been going through our photographs. Unfortunately, most of them are only of me. But one of yours slipped by ... did you know that? I am worried about you. Never before have I had such beautiful letters from you, yet I would rather have your cheerful old self again. You must not take our situation too tragically. It is after all but a time for preparation ... You look so slim and delicate in your new dress. If only I could have taken a better look. In the hurry, I couldn't see everything. If only I could see you again soon. You must not lose your joy of life. Go outside a lot. You can look at all our spots – without worrying that we shall be seen and that the gossip starts up again. But the main thing is to get out, to swim, to look after your body. Please try not to be sad when you think of me."

And here is a page from another, a very important one for me: "I have been realizing lately how much my experience of Walther lives and dies with you. Now it is again surging up within me. Or was it only all that studying that made me so dead inside? This much is certain: all my Walther pieces belong to you and will always be written for you. It is wonderful to feel so close to another person ... I have been racking my brains about what to give you to take along on your journey. But just now I have nothing ready. From Breslau I had brought you a book about the City Hall but didn't get around to sending it to you – it was left with Mali.[21] Please get it from her. You know that in all my travels I have always looked for the nicest thing I can find to bring you. I shall always do that. Mali told me so many nice, dear things about you – unfortunately not enough. If only you knew what good wishes are travelling with this letter!"

SATURDAY EVENING, 27 AUGUST

Have spent the day fixing my clothes and making other preparations for the trip. Around 4:30 I walked along the usual route. But instead of meeting you, I ran into a student from my Olmütz Quarta[22] with his parents and little brother. They were coming from the station. Said they had just inquired the way to Seegasse.[23] What a coincidence!

In the evening, Mutti and I went to the movies. Greta Garbo in *Camille*. Excellent theatre, but you are not allowed to forget for a moment that it is theatre. Mutti's heart was acting up – her usual palpitations – so we came home directly. She is still not completely all right.

When I arrived home, there was a pleasant surprise waiting for me. Our maid Friedl greeted me excitedly with "Fräulein Hanne, go and look in your room." My heart almost stood still as I hoped against any reasonable hope … It was a gorgeous bouquet of roses, delivered by the "little boy" from Olmütz. I was really pleased. I'll have to tell you about Pokorney Günther[24] another time; that little guy is one of a kind!

I wonder where you spent your evening. Perhaps also in the cinema? Perhaps we should have left by the main entrance. But since Mutti was not feeling well, we took the shortest route.

OLMÜTZ, WEDNESDAY 31 AUGUST

A big jump since my last entry: it's my first night back in Olmütz. The trip was uneventful. My suitcase was heavy, but luckily, whenever I needed to lift it or take it down, some strong-armed cavalier was ready to offer help. In Prague I took the streetcar from Masaryk to Wilson Station where I had an hour's wait. Just time to write a note to H. I then asked an attendant if there was a mailbox nearby. I didn't want to walk far with my heavy load. "Follow me," he said, with a conspiratorial wink, then picked up my case and led me via the first-class waiting room to the platform, "to make sure you get a good seat, Miss." The train – an exceptionally long one – was already standing there, although not officially ready for boarding. I posted my letter and got on. There I was, the lone occupant. Presently, the hordes began to board. Moments before departure, I saw Dr Bader hurry along the platform. He is the pesky Olmütz colleague whom I had been dodging all last year. By coincidence, he ended up in my compartment. Perhaps just as well; I had no chance of brooding about the past and agonizing over the future, and the trip passed quickly as we chatted about this and that.

My room in Samenhofova 24 awaited me, spic and span, and somewhat spruced up with a new tablecloth and freshly laundered, starched curtains, with the cords fixed so that they pull more easily. The chairs also have been repaired, and on the table stands a bunch of dahlias in a blue ceramic vase. I have unpacked and have promised myself to keep things tidy!

What will tomorrow bring? Principal Lachnit had added an exceptionally warm personal greeting to his official letter when he informed me of my reappointment and promotion.

THURSDAY, 1 SEPTEMBER

What a full and busy day! In the morning, reunion with Erna Menta. She is the good, dear friend as always. I am blessed to have a companion with whom there is so much give and take, so much sharing and intellectual stimulation. Last year we spent all our spare time together, eating, talking, laughing, biking.

Principal Lachnit, a.k.a. *der Alte* [the old man], and all the other teachers welcomed me warmly. Ressel, my appointed mentor of last year, is dancing around me importantly, having announced that he is to be my adviser again. I am to teach mostly Czech language in five different grades, ranging from the Prima to the Octava. The Prima I have for German as well, and I shall also be their home-room teacher.

There are three new additions to the staff: Freising, an attractive, apparently agreeable young woman; Schroepfer (who teaches Latin and Czech), a scholarly philologist and pedant, somewhat like Bader but not, we hope, as mean and malicious. And then there is Mück. Erna and I already had our fill of him yesterday afternoon in the coffee house. We had looked forward to an hour or so by ourselves to catch up on things, and it wasn't just that he joined us uninvited – but such pompous posturing and bluster! We were able to shake him off only by retreating to my room.

Had a delightful letter from Traudl Holub, my roommate from Prague days.

Must get to bed. It is almost midnight. Tomorrow is the first day of school. Before turning out the light: I have been looking at your picture for a long while, into those pensive, melancholy eyes. They are almost speaking to me. Remember the last time – was it only last Tuesday? – when you rounded the corner and there I suddenly stood before you? That's how you looked at me then. For as long as you dared. We knew it would have to do us for a long time.

Hanna's colleagues at the Staatsrealgymnasium in Olmütz, 1938: Principal Lachnit (*centre front*), Hanna (*behind his right shoulder*), Erna Menta (*to Hanna's right*), Bergmann (*behind Hanna's left shoulder*)

SATURDAY, 3 SEPTEMBER

A letter! At least I know that you are all right and that you have found some inner peace. It made me feel like working too, and I did. Have sketched out the first scene of our play.

The first day of school. It began with the whole school attending Mass. A festive, solemn ceremony. Several mothers waited outside the church to see their offspring parade by. Afterwards, as the classes left the church in formation, with us teachers already outside, every one of my former Quarta greeted me with a broad, beaming grin. I felt my eyes filling up. They are the fourteen year olds. I am sorry, really sorry, not to have them again this year. We had such wonderful rapport, and they responded with amazingly creative work in German composition. We also had great times producing our group recitations – reciting the poems they had memorized with various combinations of voices, alternating unison with solo parts. It was fun – for me as well as them, because I could savour being a conductor.

I gave my introductory speech to my Prima. Although most of them are eleven years old, they seem very young. As I was walking along the

street later this afternoon, one of them, breathless with running and excitement, caught up with me (he had evidently been lying in wait): "Frau
Professor, I can't get the form you told us to fill out." He then prattled
on about other things. And finally, after taking a deep breath and a side-
ways glance at me, he could contain himself no longer: "Is it true that
there will always be a girl sitting beside a boy?"

"Who gave you that idea?"

"You did."

I had cautioned them that if there was too much whispering and talking, I would make them move. My informant told me that the boys were
quite upset, vowing they would "sit beside no girl." What evidently
started this rumour was the realization that the point of a shuffle was to
separate friends; and trying to imagine whom they would least want for
a neighbour, they came up with this disturbing scenario. What a difference a few years will make!

To celebrate my promotion, my fellow teachers gave me the bumps
today.[25]

Bergmann, the phys. ed. instructor, who is a functionary of the Henlein
party,[26] told me all sorts of things about how great life is in Germany these
days.

Tomorrow is Sunday. Bergmann, Gellert, and Ernstberger[27] have invited me to go mushrooming with them. (Erna is in Brünn.)

MONDAY, 5 SEPTEMBER

The first full day of school. The little ones are really very little and naive.
One of them put up his hand: "Please, may I go to the toilet? For a big
one?" I have two Raabs in the same class, a boy and a girl, and assumed
that they were twins. But no, he is her uncle.

A sign of the seriousness of the political situation: Czechoslovak defence bonds have been issued, and urgent appeals have been made to
purchase them to "help defend the Republic." During a general staff
meeting, the faculty collectively decided not to participate. Afterwards,
Appel[28] and Bergmann came to me separately to assure me that I need
not consider their decision binding. I shall of course contribute to the

defence fund and didn't need their permission to do so. But I consider it rather decent of them to want to show me that they appreciate my position and don't wish to put me on the spot. But how sad that they all are hoping and wishing for Hitler to take over the country.

Erna and I took in a movie after school: *Mary of Scotland*, with Katharine Hepburn. An excellent film, especially with Hepburn's wonderful performance. Rarely have I seen such an expressive face (Lenore Ulric, perhaps?). Erna and I talked for a long time afterwards. Erna is a German nationalist of deep conviction and an admirer of Hitler.

Earlier today I unpacked the trunk that had arrived from home and wrote letters: to the parents, to you, and to Hanne Gottlieb, my friend from Prague days. There was no time to work on the play. It is now 8:15 PM and I am too tired for anything except perhaps some French. But I firmly intend to spend an hour every morning, from six to seven, on our "Walther."

I keep rereading your letter. Need I say how happy it makes me that you seem to be making plans involving both of us? This gives me hope and makes me want to prepare in all sorts of ways: business correspondence in English, French, and German; English shorthand; and learning to drive a car.

SATURDAY, 10 SEPTEMBER

To make everything worse, my period is overdue. I am very worried and tense. Impossible to work on "Walther." It's almost as if I were intellectually and emotionally paralysed. School takes all morning and some afternoons. Yesterday the *Klassenbuch* [class attendance book][29] had to be made up and copied. Being in charge of a Prima makes for extra work because all the information has to be gleaned from original documents.

But I had a few more laughs with my little innocents. At the outset, I had explained that no one was to leave school before classes were over without first asking permission. It's a standard rule (for their own safety or for the sake of orderly bookkeeping?). The next day I lost one pupil in mid-morning. Absences are recorded in their report cards: number of hours absent, excused, or – *horribile dictu* – not excused! Next day they lined up in front of my desk, one after the other, all except Rony.

"Please, Rony is back."

"Please, Rony thought it was already twelve o'clock" – on and on until I couldn't hide my amusement any longer and announced that the collective apology was accepted.

Thursday I had the Octava. All eyes were on the door as usual when there is a teacher entering a class for the first time. Who is it going to be? But I was not prepared for the noisy to-do that followed. Standing up, they applauded and pounded their desks and generally acted pleased.

Renewed tension in town last night. Local demonstrations by the Henleins[30] are expected and the children have a 7 PM curfew.

I finished a French book and started an English one. Not nearly enough.

SUNDAY, 11 SEPTEMBER

Very early – still in bed. I have been getting up at 5:30 AM. In the evenings, I can't keep my eyes open.

Erna told me that when the baker delivered bread in the military barracks yesterday, they said he'd better begin to say goodbye to his children and start polishing his marching boots. Within days, "things will begin to happen." I am in a quandary. Do I pass the warning on to H? I am scared to give advice. Suppose he runs from the Czechs – and the Austrians put him in uniform?

TUESDAY, 13 SEPTEMBER

What a day it has been! An emotional roller coaster. First of all, wonderful mail. A letter from you and a separate package of manuscripts. "Notenbuch für Maria Hav"[31] – some of the songs you set to the poems of Walther von der Vogelweide which I had "translated" for you into modern German, and one song with words by the English poet John Masefield, which I had also shown you. Can you possibly have any idea how happy you have made me? I am dreaming what it would be like if we could work openly together.

But then, this evening at Erna's, I heard Hitler's big speech from Nuremberg. More threatening and terrifying than ever. Numb with fear and worry, I have now been back in my room for half an hour. I have never done this before, but like a child I actually knelt by my bed and prayed.

I wonder where you are. Who knows when and where – and if – we shall see each other again. I fear that the days of the Czechoslovak Republic are numbered. Will that at least mean peace? Surely, if we survive it, things can only get better. Except for the Jews. What will happen to us?

All week, too tense and worried to work on our play, I have been agonizing where I would go if war broke out. Olmütz is a garrison town and would be a battleground. In which direction would I run? To Prossnitz with its sizable Jewish community, as Mr Altar advises? (Mr Altar is the father of the only Jewish student in my class.) Into the Czech interior, which would be occupied? Bergmann is trying to persuade me to go to Müglitz, into the relative safety of what he thinks will be the German hinterland. He wants to give me a letter from the Henlein party, a free passage of sorts offering safe conduct. What would he say? That I have been a devoted teacher of German literature and am a decent person? That I am the proverbial one Jewish friend who is the exception?

WEDNESDAY, 14 SEPTEMBER

This is the day of decision about the fate of the republic. I have packed all my documents, letters, and photographs, and have taken out what money I have in the savings bank. Within the next hour, Bergmann said, I will hear from his party partner Baier (whom I have never met) whether war has broken out. Meanwhile in school this morning there was supposed to have been an assembly honouring Masaryk, our founding president, but all we heard on the radio were crackling noises and static.

Bergmann came over to where I sat and said, very solemnly, "The time has come to say goodbye." He will, of course, depart for Germany. Having played a part in helping to break up the republic, he expects to be welcomed and rewarded there. Before he spoke to me, I had no idea

Notenbuch

für Maria Hav

4 Lieder nach altdeutschen Texten

für tiefe Stimme und Klavier

von

Hans Feiertag

1. Im Maien
2. Als der Sommer kommen war . . .
3. Es stand in voller Weisse . . .
4. Ich sass auf einem Seine . . .
5. Beauty

Title page of "Notenbuch für Maria Hav." For safety, Feiertag's name was not on it originally. I added it later.

"Im Maien" was one of the first *Vogelweide Lieder* composed by Hans Feiertag; text translated into modern German by Hanna Fischl.

that the situation had reached such a critical point – that the Czech government had turned down Henlein's ultimatum, that seven age groups
have been called up, and that in Germany troops are on the move.

After clearing out my bank account, I went to the post office to place
a call to the parents, but was told that all lines to Komotau have been
taken over by the military. I ran home, where I found Erna waiting for
me. Back to the post office to send telegrams – but where to? Where is
everybody? I sent duplicates, one to Komotau (asking them to wire me
their whereabouts) and one, by general delivery, to Beroun, where my
paternal grandmother used to live. I was grasping at straws. What made
me think that any of these would reach them? I tried to telephone
again, this time calling it "express," and within three minutes I had a
connection. No one answered. Of course not. Thank goodness, it
meant that they had flown the coop. But where are they? I should have
known that they will contact me as soon as they can, but I felt I needed
to do something.

Back in my room, I found a letter from Mutti and Mimi saying that
they are ready to leave. I am still hoping that the worst will not happen.
In the park opposite my window, children are playing as usual. Yet
planes are flying overhead, and the town is abuzz with soldiers. I wonder
if they know any better than I do what they should do. The guns are
loaded and it is all very frightening.

THURSDAY, 15 SEPTEMBER

We are not only still alive but we are pretty cheerful. Having taken leave
of Bergmann yesterday with a solemn farewell, we met this morning in
the staffroom as usual. As of 5 PM yesterday, the situation has been ap-
preciably less tense. Chamberlain is going to visit Hitler. On the other
hand, Henlein added fresh tension by calling on the Sudeten Germans
to offer resistance. Against what? Such posturing! All the same, I now
have some hope that war may yet be avoided; except for the civil war –
the war of nerves – that has been going on for some time.

Yes, I am calm and cheerful now that I don't have to make a decision!
Meanwhile, a telegram has come from the parents, telling me that they

are in Nova Hut pod Nizborem – I presume because Mutti's cousin Mařena Jelinek lives there. As well, Altar, the Jewish student in my Octava, came to me during recess with a message from his father saying I should come to them if there is an emergency. Furthermore, Principal Lachnit informed me that my *Dekret* – the official documentation of my new rank – has arrived from the ministry. For how long will that be of use to me? I must have said something to this effect because Lachnit took a long look at me and said in his slow, ponderous way, "But Frau Colleague, don't be afraid. I have often been told by the others what a lovable, nice girl you are, and the students also are fond of you. After all, we take into account what sort of person we are dealing with."[32]

Did my laundry. Now I shall tackle the play. Won't try to make copies of the songs. How do I know that tomorrow I won't have to put everything into the fire anyway?

Little Karl Stanzel came to the staffroom saying that the lady teacher had accidentally taken his notebook. I was assumed to be the guilty party and was summoned to the door. He took one look at me, turned red as a beet, and stammered, "Please, I mean the historymadamteacher" (namely, Frau Freising, his *Geschichtsfraulehrerin*). Why should I find that so hilarious? Hasn't he just done what Germans have always done – creating monster compounds by stringing words together?

Where are you?

FRIDAY, 23 SEPTEMBER

What a week! What we are experiencing personally are historic events of global importance.[33] The situation has been changing from hour to hour, each piece of news out of date almost as soon as it is published, with wild rumours running ahead of every event. Finally, yesterday, there was great rejoicing that peace has been preserved, albeit at a high price. But today clouds are gathering again, ever more threatening. The tension is almost unbearable. Parents have kept their children at home – there have, on average, been no more than five students in a class. To try and concentrate on teaching is torture. But it is a good way to control my nerves. In my spare time I am furiously learning English and for the last two days have been starting on Swedish. It seemed at first rather difficult, but I am slowly gaining confidence. At least I no longer read a page over and over again without knowing what I have read. If only I survive the year! No word from H.

Colleague Suchanek[34] said today, "Is your husband in town?" In response to what must have been a surprised and puzzled lift of my eyebrows, he repeated the question. My expression evidently became even more stupid, and he finally shrugged his shoulders: "It was just a joke." Was it? Or was it a fishing expedition? Has the Olmütz rumour mill been working overtime? Nowadays, everything is so weird that hardly anything surprises one any more.

Yesterday, school was dismissed in mid-morning because of a demonstration. Freising spent the afternoon with me before taking the four o'clock train to her home in Prerau. She is five months pregnant. On leaving, she invited me to her home, very warmly, "even for a longer period, should it become necessary." Most kind of her. They all seem to realize that my position is more precarious than anyone else's around here. Unlike me, they have a home, somewhere, and know what camp they belong to … Hella was also here and invited me to her parents' place in Bärn, north of here – which would become part of Germany. But for the time being I have decided to remain here.

Bergmann is said to be visiting his ailing mother. Mück, Freising, and Wohlfahrtstädter were simply absent today. Everything is a great muddle. I called on Captain Garner to see about my English lessons, but he wasn't at home. I shall try again. The students have been boycotting Schroepfer's classes. She is said to be "a red." We have been ordered to cover our windows at night and maintain a blackout. Our nerves are so taut that every sound makes us wonder whether this is it. I have had a sleepless night, half sick with worry.

Dear diary, you see how disjointed and muddled my report is. But right now, in the middle of events, how can I sift the important from the trivial? What is temporary? If I had reported all the waves of fear and hope that I have experienced during the last few days, it would seem like a miracle that I am as calm as I am and able to study new languages. You must forgive me that I find it impossible to work on our "Walther von der Vogelweide" script. What I should really be doing is give an accounting to myself of my past life ...

Somewhere in the house the radio is on, and through the wall I hear the mobs shouting – people roaring like animals. What a world! Everyone afraid of everyone else; hatred and distrust everywhere.

If only we could be together! I feel desperately alone. My bag with documents and photographs is packed.

SATURDAY, 24 SEPTEMBER

General mobilization has been ordered. I spent all morning with errands. Visited Čedok, bought bread, called on Frau Ressel. Excitement everywhere as people cluster on the streets in agitated conversation, while recruits with their suitcases make their way to the station or to barracks, and their women stand there, waving after them, weeping. I saw one young woman run back and forth, ringing her hands and sobbing, and finally collapsing on the street.

Later today I am supposed to acquire a gas mask. They were sold out this morning, but another shipment is expected. People on the street are already carrying them. They look like the *Botanisierbüchsen*, the specimen cans we toted to carry our botanical treasures when we were young. Colleagues Gellert and Schenk have been called up. Most people are leaving.

Half an hour later. According to the German news, there is still hope for peace. I shall continue reading my English book and later on will try to call on Captain Garner for another lesson.

I just heard a shot. And two more. Dear God, let people realize that life is precious and death final!

A beautifully sunny, warm autumn. How we used to enjoy these days! And now we are pleased about every hour that has passed safely. Burghardt has returned and greeted me with an exclamation of how well I look. Principal Lachnit has invited me to take shelter in his basement if it proves necessary. A troop of recruits just marched by. What a world!

Evening of the same day. I bought the gas mask. A long letter from Papa – the first ever! The first long one, I mean. Usually he just adds his greetings to Mutti's, with the comment that she has already given all the news. (She usually has.) He has much to report. Louis and Maňa are leaving for Brussels and from there will continue to Canada. They have given us their four-room apartment in Kralupy, including furniture. That's great news. Without a home and means of support, what would Papa and Mutti do?

In the afternoon, I went once more to town. In front of a weapons shop there was suddenly a commotion: first the sound of breaking glass, then a woman screaming. Within seconds a small crowd had gathered. As I came closer, I saw a legionnaire bleeding from nose and mouth, standing in the centre, looking dazed. The good man had walked into the door thinking it was open. A small event. Somehow, everything becomes magnified because everyone is on the brink of hysteria.

Pachl, the assistant janitor, rang his boss at midnight to say that he is taking his vacation now and is leaving town. Lachnit was quite cross; Pachl is not of military age.

Good night, my dear. What will the morrow bring?

I almost forgot: no school tomorrow. The building is being taken over by four hundred (Czech) soldiers. Mr Kassal just told me that Austria has called up ten years of reserves. I don't want to believe it, but the fear has got hold of me now and won't let go. I saw many soldiers today taking leave of their girls.

SUNDAY, 25 SEPTEMBER

A brilliant autumn day. Did some laundry this morning, then sat in the park with my English book. The noon news was rather comforting. The peace barometer seems to be rising and my heart leapt with joy.

After an opulent meal of soup, chicken, potatoes, and dessert, I went to Erna's. We went on a bike trip – for the first time in a long while – and it felt good. Yesterday we almost fled in panic, and today we are riding around in the sunshine, peacefully and happily. We travelled along a beautiful road at first, but by and by it became rough and miserable, finally almost petering out into a narrow, bumpy path. We pushed our bikes uphill, curious where we would end up, and arrived at the Neretein airport. The few planes parked there looked like lame grasshoppers. One tried to take off but seemed glued to the ground and just went round in a circle. When it came dangerously close to where we stood, we got a bit scared and retreated.

We had just returned home when Mr Hlinka – Erna's landlord – reported that there was bad news. "Hitler is going to speak tomorrow. Something must be wrong." Gone was our happy mood. I wonder whether I should not after all go to the parents. In case of war, Olmütz is bound to be bombed. But if I leave, how can H find me? I have no idea where he is.

So, for the time being, I'll await developments. I have not befriended my gas mask yet. It sits in the cupboard in the box in which I bought it. Shall try to work on "Walther" tomorrow.

MONDAY, 26 SEPTEMBER

Erna came to my room and chased me out of bed for an early morning walk – it was such a lovely morning. Then there was a mad rush doing sundry errands: to school, to the post office, to various stores. Since the Czech crown is expected to drop in value, I spent what savings I had on a diamond ring (2450 crowns). Hitler's memorandum to the Czechoslovak Republic was made public, and I am convinced that the republic will not accept his conditions. This is to be the day of Hitler's speech. I am scared.

Shall I go to my parents? Here I feel as if I am sitting on a powder keg.

TUESDAY, 27 SEPTEMBER

Hitler spoke last night. I heard it at Erna's. In her view, "he is the man of the century" and "what he says sounds simple but is profound." I can't see how our republic can accept his demands. He argues that for the sake of peace, the Germans gave up Alsace-Lorraine, South Tyrol, and the Polish Corridor, and now it is the turn of the Czechs to sacrifice the

Sudetenland. But is there not a considerable difference in these two "sacrifices"? The Germans, defeated in 1918, had no choice. The Czechs are being asked to give up an integral part of their country voluntarily.

Bought a hat box (to carry my documents, etc.), then went to the station to check train times. What incredible confusion and bedlam! No one has any idea what is going on. I am going to the parents after all, until Sunday. That's when Hitler's ultimatum expires. Then we'll know whether it is to be war or peace. Lachnit refused to give me permission to leave for a few days. As if it mattered! There is no school anyway. I am now determined to go. My train leaves at 3:30 in the morning. Will I ever see Olmütz again?

Later. A few days have gone by since my last entry – fateful days of weird happenings and historic twists. But to go back to last Tuesday, I spent the evening with the Kassals.[35] They offered me supper, but I had no appetite and a pain in my stomach signalled that I was coming down with *Reisefieber* [the nervous excitement before a journey].

It was pitch-dark as I walked to the streetcar at 11 PM; mandatory blackout. That's why I wanted to go early and wait in the station restaurant, perhaps even doze a little. I was expecting the usual deserted station but found the place bustling with crowds and noise and confusion. Fortunately, there was still an empty table and I could at least sit down. Four more hours to wait! All around me were men in uniform, mostly officers. One of them joined me and soon we were engaged in conversation. About the political situation, naturally. Impossible to think or talk about anything else. He was convinced that war was inevitable. Our conversation was interrupted by the announcement that a train for Prague, which was an hour and a half overdue, was expected to pull in shortly. Lucky me! Perhaps I could even snatch a bit of sleep on the train.

The train was in complete darkness. Before taking a seat, one had to ask whether it was occupied. So I sat there, tense, wide awake, firmly clutching my purse and the hat box. At one point, a detachment of soldiers trooped onto the train, half-frozen from guard duty. They filled every niche of the coach with their bodies and their noise (standing room only by that time) and got off at the next station. All in pitch darkness. Spooky. Later I went into second class (from the third where I belonged), where there was some light. Beside me sat an air force officer who was exuding information: "Either Hitler gives in or there will be war" … "With our first-rate defence system, we can take on Germany on our own" … "Our fortifications are stronger than the Maginot Line" … "Many Russian planes have arrived here already in support" … "Because the German generals are opposed to war at this stage, Hitler had eight of them shot." (Which reminds me: earlier today, Erna brought me the news that Hitler had shot Goering in the leg – which was the "sickness" that caused his absence at the Nuremberg Rally.) "You don't have to be afraid," said the air force officer. "Just remember what I told you today, on 28 September." He also said that the promised surrender of certain areas and the change of the Hodža[36] regime were only a trick. There should be no question of giving up even an inch of Czechoslovak soil. And even if the government did yield, "the army would not obey." He got off in Pardubice.

The train finally arrived in Prague at 9 AM. There were Sokol[37] scouts with red arm bands, nurses, and soldiers patrolling with fixed bayonets. Hardly any cars in sight, only people – downcast, worried, glum-looking people. Some windows taped or boarded over crosswise to protect against bomb damage. Many people carrying gas masks.

At Wilson Station. The next train towards Nova Hut pod Nizborem not until 12:30. I call Aunt Ottla.[38] Hanuš answers. His father – Uncle Max – is rather poorly and is being taken to a clinic. What is my opinion of the political situation?

"I don't believe there will be war," I venture.

Hanuš: "So you think they will hand him everything? Whether they do or not, I believe he will march all the way into Prague without a shot being fired."

Next I call the Auerbachs.[39] Mrs A invites me to come and see them but is sorry she can't send the car to pick me up at the streetcar – they are short of gas. It was a bit of a climb from the end of the line to the villa, but I did want to see them and also to pick up her promised letter of reference, which I might need soon. So up I trudged. It was hot. Imagine me, weary and dirty, in my winter coat, carrying the heavy hat box, which I hadn't wanted to deposit at the station along with my suitcase.

At the Auerbachs, pessimism and worry. The house full of relations, refugees from all directions. Every five minutes I discover yet another one: grandmother and grandfather, Uncle Paul from Vienna, Editka and Gerti, Benno Pollak. I know them all from my days with the family. Daža and Max are in America. Norbert is downtown; he was on "night duty." Olga Auerbach has the letter ready for me. I drink a cup of tea, chat a little with everybody, and run down to the streetcar. Back at the station, more waiting; and milling crowds and chaos.

My neighbour on the train was a woman who cried all the way to Beroun. Her husband had been called up. The two men opposite discussed "the situation." You no longer see a smiling face. Change of trains in Beroun with a two-hour wait. The station was crowded and all seats occupied. Behind me an old man was holding forth: "As soon as it starts, I'll pick up a weapon and join the killing. We'll do away with them all, those German swine. They'll get nothing from us, nothing. Who needs the English and French? We can do it on our own. What sort of soldier is an Englishman, anyway? And the Germans, without proper equipment? Those 75 million that Hitler talks about! Why, 40 million of them are women, half of the rest are children, and what is left? Twenty German men for every Czech. That's nothing, with our weapons! We won't be waiting around long. We'll attack them, and in no time we'll be in Berlin." The others listened attentively and nodded agreement while one of them kept repeating, "Exactly. That's precisely what I think."

On the train to Nova Hut the woman opposite me carried a huge backpack, apparently containing all her belongings. A refugee. So this is Nova Hut. I asked the way to the Jelineks – to Mutti's cousin Mařena and family – and a kind woman led me there. Mutti was of course surprised when I walked in and obviously delighted, but even she couldn't muster a smile. Papa was not there. He had returned to Komotau to arrange about sending our furniture. The apartment here consists of two tiny rooms and a windowless kitchen. Everything is topsy-turvy, indescribably chaotic.

The Jelinek boys[40] are sweet. Real boys. The little one is in the Secunda; Hanuš in the Octava. There is also Jarka, a classmate of Hanuš, very bright but very anaemic-looking, whom they have taken in as a third son. Mimi is here as well as Aunt Milly and Ruth, and later in the evening we were surprised by Aunt Antschi's arrival. Milly and Antschi are very depressed and do a lot of complaining and wailing. Mutti, of course, is no less worried, but she seems to have more self-control.

FRIDAY, 30 SEPTEMBER

This morning it was announced that we are giving up the Sudeten, thus preserving "peace in our time." Peace! It makes it possible to believe that there may be a future for us after all.[41] Above all, you don't have to go to war. Soon I may even know where you are. Everyone around me is feeling low. Would they really have preferred war to a truncated country? At last, after a nightmare that lasted almost a year, we are able to relax, knowing there will not be a war.

Saturday a telegram arrived from Erna, saying that to receive my salary cheque I have to be there in person. So the "old man" forces me to return after all. Which I would have done anyway. I am leaving on the 10:30 train – by daylight this time! But no one knows whether there will be a connecting train in Beroun for Prague or one in Prague for Olmütz. The station master said that I should expect to arrive in Olmütz within two or three days! I couldn't tell whether he was joking. He was not smiling. The Jelinek children accompanied me to the station and handed me a bouquet of roses.

It was a very long train. I counted thirty coaches – military transport – but I managed to get a seat. The other occupants of the compartment were Czech railway workers fleeing from Komotau,[42] with their belongings stuffed into knapsacks, bags, and bundles. In Beroun, everybody and everything had to get off the train, spilling out onto the platform. Never have I seen such a mess of baskets, suitcases, trunks, bedding, parcels, knapsacks, and bundles, with women, children, and old men standing and sitting between and on top, either talking politics (what else?) or weeping, or blankly staring into space. Everyone desperately tired. And if someone else were to describe the scene, it would probably include a young woman with a big bouquet of roses.

I was in fact trying to imagine some of the "case histories" of my travelling companions. Why was that woman over there suddenly starting to shout, almost hysterically? Three German-speaking women from Bodenbach [like Komotau, a very German town], now returning home, seemed worried about how they would be received. Had they "backed the wrong horse" and run away? Or perhaps they were Social Democrats and would be branded as "red."

In Prague similar scenes. Refugees in groups, in queues, and singly; some noisy and some very still. How can this little country, now amputated and impoverished, receive and support them? What will become of me? How can I hope to go abroad now that I am a refugee in my own country? Uncle Louis didn't make it either. On the day that he was to leave, mobilization was declared and all exits shut tight.

Arrived in Olmütz at 1:30 AM. The Kassals were still up. Mrs K had been allowed to pick up my cheque after all. A card from Dr Losova – she wants me to continue the lessons. Nothing from H.

SUNDAY, 2 OCTOBER

School still occupied by the military. I visited Erna. She is of course jubilant. But she is also beginning to sound rather unfair and fanatical. Very critical of the Czechs while idealizing her own people. It was Erna who told Lachnit that I had gone away, and he was very cross.

MONDAY, 3 OCTOBER, EARLY MORNING

I wrote to the parents asking them to ask Uncle Louis whether he would consider taking me along. In Prague I posted an inquiry after H to Mali.[43] Greetings! I feel as if there is daylight inside me again and I can think more clearly. Will tackle the play. But first I have to drop in at school, have my passport extended (if that is possible), and see Captain Garner re English lessons.

I wonder where and how you are. What might you be doing at this moment? Are you still sound asleep, with your nose in the pillows? Or sitting in front of your cup of coffee already, blond hair standing up, eyes still half closed? Are you wondering where I am?

TUESDAY, 4 OCTOBER, NOON

Worked on some English translation. Went to school. At first the guard wouldn't let me in, but eventually he allowed me to pass. I subsequently learned that I was the only one who had got through.

Have been working on the letter to Klima and wrote one to Uncle Charles.[44] He, after all, is an experienced colleague in Pilsen and may have some advice. Is Pilsen part of the Sudeten? Which reminds me, how are they going to draw the lines? There are so many bilingual border towns, like Pilsen and Olmütz.

WEDNESDAY, 5 OCTOBER

The radio just carried President Beneš's farewell.[45] The way is now cleared for a Czech brand of Fascism. Next, I am sure, will come an announcement that it is all the fault of the Jews.

Talking to me this morning, the principal said that if he were in my shoes, he would opt for Germany. Does he know what that means? We talked for a long time and once again, as so often before, he assured me of his respect and affection, and repeated that as long as he is here, I need not be afraid. He even revealed that recently, when the Sudetendeutsche Erzieherschaft [Sudeten German Teachers' Association] was organized, Baier[46] as well as my colleagues expressed regret that they could not include me. Baier even approached Lachnit with the inquiry whether I was not at least "50 percent." In which case he would have admitted me. Of course, I had no idea of any of this at the time.

In the staffroom I had a chat with Ressel. He maintained that the Jews in the Reich are not as badly treated as I think and accused me of swallowing *Greuelpropaganda* [horror stories of atrocities]. The idiot! For once, I really got mad and let him have it. No doubt that as a Jew living in Germany I wouldn't starve, but how could I live there, knowing that

I would be considered some kind of lesser creature, not just subhuman but vermin? That I would not be able to attend a theatre or concert or cinema. Or be allowed to sit on a public bench or walk in the park, or to live where I liked, befriend whomever I liked, or own property or a business. And not be able to get a fair hearing when I was unjustly treated. Who would wish to join such a state?

It has been a gorgeous autumn day, and I spent a long time walking in the park. Thinking mostly about our "Walther" project. The more I think about him, the better I understand the historic Walther. But somehow I can't make the story come to life. Is it because of the nerve-racking times that I feel so singularly unimaginative, if not barren? I so much *need* to be able to manage it – for you, for us! But reading over what I have written so far, I find the conversations and people wooden, and the plot petty and trivial. And boring. Yet I imagine Walther as someone who takes an almost childlike pleasure in ordinary things and radiates a joyful exuberance. A straight, guileless person, yet one who perceives the essential and recognizes the important issues. Childlike also in his simplicity, yet mature in his judgment. Very concerned with public affairs and the state of the world, fighting for the cause of the German Kaiser against a bartering, manipulative pope. Someone who knows how to speak clearly, plainly, and forcefully but is thwarted by hostile intrigues. Personally sensitive and vulnerable, unable to look after his own interests. Admired and listened to by many, but homeless and financially insecure – a beggar, really, who depends on the court's charity. Because his sweetheart is a peasant girl, his enemies at court pursue him with malicious gossip that leaves him helpless and exposed.

Are these the traits of the historic Walther or of my own Herr Walther? Probably a blend of both. But did you not yourself write to tell me, three months ago almost to the day, that your Walther experience "lives and dies" with me and that all your Walther pieces belong to me and will always be written for me?

I feel so lonesome. It is a month since I heard, since that very special parcel came. The more I think about its contents, the more significant it seems: "Walther – Lieder" in a rather complete little cycle, symbolic of our relationship, plus a recently added song based on a poem by the

English poet laureate. Dedicated to Maria Hav. Their symbolic relevance aside, these songs are very, very beautiful. Some of the most tuneful you have written.

Why don't I hear from you? Or does your mail not reach me? Everyone complains of frayed nerves. All seem at the end of their tether, the reaction to the tension of the last few days.

THURSDAY, 6 OCTOBER

According to the agreement, the inhabitants of the Sudeten will have the choice (individually) of opting for Germany or Czechoslovakia. Most likely they will opt with their feet!

The day was spent with errands: passport office, having my photograph taken, another attempt to reach Captain Garner (who will not be back for another week). On the advice of Schroepfer who, along with her husband, doesn't wish to join the Reich either, I drafted a letter to Klima – the man at the Ministry of Education in charge of placements.

I read a legend by Kolbenheyer,[47] "God's Justification." Very beautiful: Man was created in order to break through the seven rings that surround all things. From the volume *Drei Legenden*. I also looked in at the school. The director did not refer to my having been AWOL but merely inquired after my parents and asked whether I had received my cheque. In contrast to his usual calm self, he seemed rather nervous or distracted. Our school is now housing German soldiers [that is, German-speaking Czechoslovak soldiers], who refused to be armed. All other schools, according to a radio communiqué, will resume instruction tomorrow.

SUNDAY, 9 OCTOBER

Still no news from you or about you. Mail with the border areas and with abroad has been cut off. Mutti writes that Uncle Louis and family have flown to Strasbourg. The parents are moving to Kralupy.

I bought books on English and French commercial correspondence and am settling down to business. A new world for me. I am working with both languages more or less simultaneously. The sample letters have the same content in both, and it is interesting to compare the different styles and attitudes in the two, or rather three, idioms. As well, I

Feiertag in the Austrian Alps, 1935

am reading Bernard Shaw and Proust. Have also been working on "Walther." It is getting a little easier, though I do have to force myself. My imagination still leaves much to be desired.

Spent time in the coffee house several days in a row to read the papers instead of eating lunch. I have the feeling that these are historic times. Has it ever happened in world history that a state has voluntarily relinquished part of its territory? Poor Czechoslovakia is being attacked and exploited unfairly. The Germans are now claiming even purely Czech places, using the excuse that their annexation is necessary for some technical or strategic reason – railway lines, for example. But where this would work in favour of Czechoslovakia, nationality is deemed to be the determining factor. The mainline Prague-Brünn-Kosice railway, which runs through Olmütz, is cut in two places.

School is to resume tomorrow, but we have some guests at school: police from the border areas. Parallel classes are to be merged. I have only one class tomorrow: German in the Prima. Erna has left, as of two days ago. For Müglitz? I hope she'll come back.

All sorts of rumours are circulating about the fate of Olmütz. Some people are expecting the German army to arrive on the twelfth, and they claim that Czech soldiers are already moving to Prossnitz; others believe that Olmütz will remain Czech. That is what I think too. After all, the surrounding area – the hinterland – is solidly Czech, and so is the majority of the population in the town itself. Our Germans, on the other hand, are convinced that it will be annexed and are already throwing their weight around.

Later. It is now 4 PM and I have been working on "Walther." Shall now do some studying. Good afternoon! You must be all right because I am feeling rather good and cheerful for no discernible reason. But please, please write! And I wonder why Mali[48] is not answering. Is she not at home? Did mail go astray? Or has she stopped writing to me as well? What a world! It's incredible that one man can bring so much unhappiness to millions of people, with one stroke cutting off their lifeline.

MONDAY, 10 OCTOBER

Good evening! Except that it's not a good evening. I have been sitting here for almost an hour, my head on the table, weeping helplessly. The realization of our whole miserable situation overwhelmed me. Where are you? What sense is there in waiting? For what? Is there a way home for us? I realize now just what you were willing to sacrifice for me. Are you still prepared to leave with me? And if you do, won't you regret it?

We have now been separated almost a year, bound only by our memories. Wouldn't it be best if we ended it, tried to cut the bond? For you, it would mean that doors would open. As for me, I would muddle along somehow. At least I would not have to worry about emigrating, of going who knows where. Yet I can't bear the thought. Shall try to work on the play.

Spoke to Mr Proksch and some other Germans. They expect the German army to arrive here within two days. The Czech National Bank has already moved, they say, and the airfield has been cleared. And they are well prepared with a good supply of flags, arm bands, placards, and garlands.

I was sitting in the staffroom, feeling something like this,

Ich sass auf einem Steine
und deckte Bein mit Beine,
drauf setzte ich den Ellenbogen.
Ich hatt in meine Hand geschmogen
das Kinn und auch die Wange.
Da dachte ich gar lange,
wie man in dieser Welt sollt leben,[49]

when I felt a hand lightly stroking my hair and heard the principal's voice behind me: "Don't be sad. Fate tumbles us about, but we don't get lost. Everything will turn out all right." At that point old Colleague Just came in. After Lachnit left, he said in his homey dialect, very much in contrast to Lachnit's lofty little speech: "What was that he said about fate? Sure, bad things happen. Easily." I had to laugh.

Our staffroom contingent is thinning out more and more. Missing: Burghardt, Bergmann, Freising, Mück, Wohlfahrtstädter, Zapletal, Rozehnal, Gotschlich, Gellert, Schenk.[50]

I am torturing myself with these business letters. Made hardly any progress today. While I am working with the French text, I forget the English, and vice versa.

Still the tenth! An hour later. After I had a good cry, I tackled the play – with gusto. I made a little – a very little – headway, but I am feeling much better now. See, I have even drawn some more ladybugs! Our sign of good times and good luck. The legs are a bit long, but that may not be a bad thing nowadays: they may be needed!

Remember the special letter paper you made for me? On *Büttenpapier* [handmade paper]. With your designs of our various symbols: ladybug, walking boots, number thirteen encased by a heart. Of course

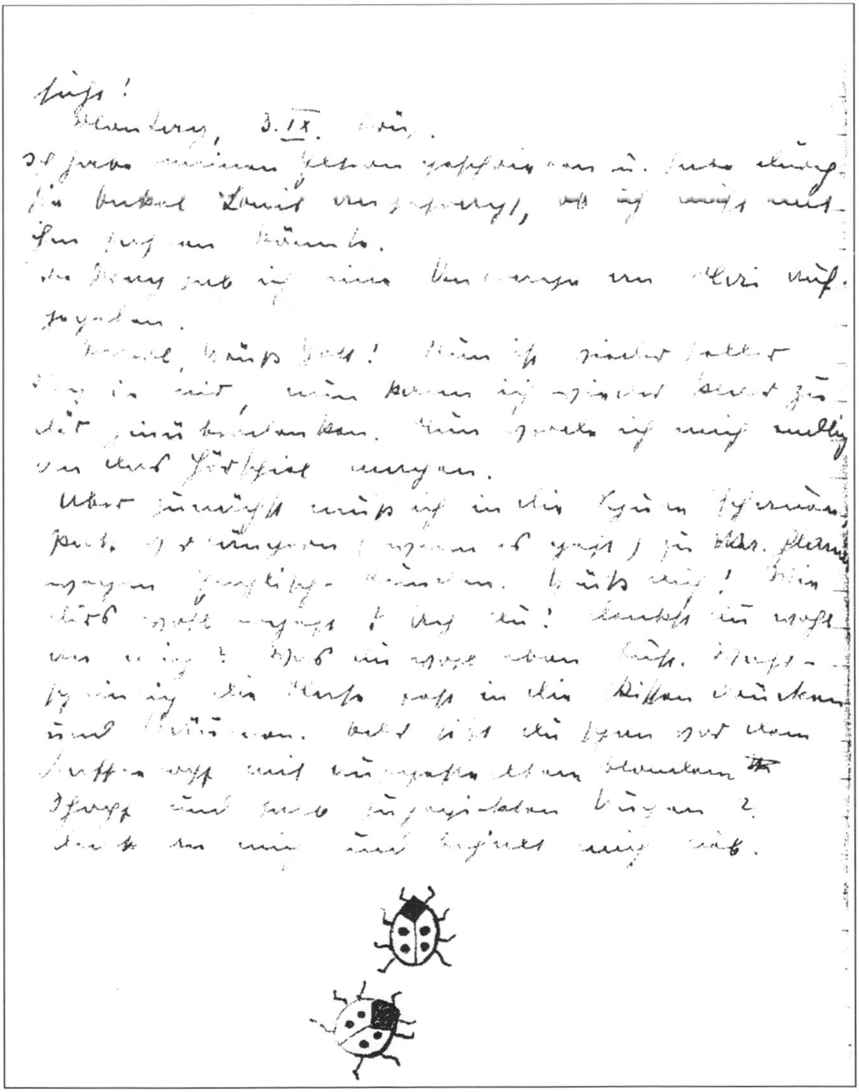

Page from the journal, with ladybugs

Feiertag with conductor Hermann Scherchen, Vienna, 1936

you remember. I still have it. The way things look, I won't use it up for a long time to come![51] I am also inserting a copy of my recent photo. It turned out quite well. Do you recognize the gentian around my neck?

TUESDAY, 11 OCTOBER
My period started today. So that was the reason for last night's misery! It is eerie how body and mind are merged. Of course we know that it is so, but we still get a shock when we are reminded of the fact that we don't know where the dividing line is between the physical and spiritual. Or is there one? I feel lousy. Cramps! And shivering with cold, like a dog. Shall crawl back to bed and take my English word lists with me. That's all I have the energy for.

THURSDAY, 13 OCTOBER
Still no news. Except a letter from Uncle Charles, but that is not the news I mean. Yesterday I worked on the play, and now I am sitting at the

table ready to continue. You should see me. I am wearing a woollen dress over my training suit, plus a grey cardigan and my housecoat. Despite the sunny autumn day, it is beastly cold in here. My room faces north. If ever I rent a room again, I shall make sure it faces the sun.

I can't get away from my memories; from our memories. They seem to tug at me, asking me, "Is that you, the same you who was there when ... Remember *Rigoletto* and the night that followed – our first night together? And the week in the tiny apartment in Vienna that we nicknamed Burg? And at the Opera? And at the Grünerts in Obergurgl? And the spot above the second big fir? Or at the little brook? And remember the evening on the Leopoldsteiner See? The nights in Hallstatt and Ebensee, in Liebshausen and Prague and Brünn? Was that really me?" Today I can walk along the streets of Olmütz and nothing shows, nothing in me shouts and radiates for everyone to see.

FRIDAY, 14 OCTOBER

A card from Mutti. They have moved to Kralupy. Whatever Erna and I talk about these days, we invariably end up with "the Jewish problem." She is trying to persuade me to go to Germany and teach in a Jewish school. Since Jews are barred from public schools, there must be special arrangements for them, and she is convinced that this would be the place for me.

Have been hard at work on "Walther." At times I quite like the result, and at times I think it's garbage – without internal structure, just a string of scenes, loosely connected, a vehicle for the songs. Which after all is its purpose – to provide continuity for the songs and to present their historical and biographical basis. But quite apart from historical accuracy, if only I could produce a lively, realistic, interesting figure of Walther! The cold makes it impossible for me to continue here. I shall take a book and sit in the park in the sun.

It seems almost certain now that Olmütz will remain Czech. Which means that our school will cease to exist. I am really curious what will happen to me. For the moment I feel almost detached, waiting for events to unfold.

Picnic, Hans and Hanna, 1936

SUNDAY, 16 OCTOBER

I took some pictures today with the self-timer, as I promised you I would. Yesterday someone from the ministry – Landesschulrat Dostal – was on the line talking to Lachnit. I asked whether I could speak to him, and did: Was there any point in my coming to Brünn for an interview? The answer was no. For the time being, our school still exists. If there is any change, they'll let me know.

Worked some more on "Walther." Unfortunately, I can't stand it indoors for long – am almost shrivelled up with cold.

TUESDAY, 18 OCTOBER

Again the park is luring me outside. The trees are exceptionally colourful this year, and the brilliant sunshine seems to call forth a last burst of life. I am reminded of Stefan George's poem "Komm in den totgesagten Park und schau."[52] But first, a quick report. The draft of "Walther" is finished – for the time being, anyway. Of course, I'm not satisfied with it. Perhaps after I let it rest for a while I'll have some fresh ideas.

Nothing new. From time to time a great sadness comes over me. But I am managing to appear quite normal. Erna picks me up at 5 PM every day and we go for a long walk. These two hours pass in animated conversation.

4 PM. I had just returned from the park – it was getting cool – when the bell went. Herta Weiss, one of my students, stood in the door with a beautiful bouquet.

THURSDAY, 20 OCTOBER

Dear diary, I really must complain about the unfairness of it all. Today, Burghardt, Mück, Zapletal, and Wohlfahrtstädter turned up again, having learned that there were no jobs for them in the Three-Thousand-Year Reich. They are now expecting to be reinstated, thus making those of us who stayed here (the two Schroepfers, Ernstberger, and myself) redundant.

More rumours. The roles are to be reversed. All of Czechoslovakia will join the German Reich, and the Czechs will be granted autonomy! It feels like an earthquake. In Schroepfer's Septima, one boy packed up his things in the middle of class, raised his arm with a "Heil Hitler," and marched out. According to the others, he did it only to annoy her. It makes me sick. Erna thought it was a good joke.

And Burghardt! With her red high heels and matching lipstick, snake leather gloves, and fancy outfits! Dancing around Lachnit, her future father-in-law, now that she has decided that his son is good enough for her after all. What a mean world! Erna and I were sitting in the park last evening when a couple strolled by, arm in arm. We recognized Mr Weiss, Herta's father, with some blonde Fräulein. And Frau Weiss is one of the nicest women.

Tried in vain to get a book to teach me English shorthand. Perhaps my German Gutenberg symbols can be applied to English. It would be my own personal code! (It works.)

Dr Bergmann has been assigned to a school in Plan.

I am reading a cute little book. In German, for a change, and rather relaxing, *Nanni Gschaftelhuber* [Nanni Busybody].[53] It reminds me of H's mother. Mrs Feiertag would have loved it. I was talking to Erna about her today.

FRIDAY, 21 OCTOBER

You may laugh about me today, dear diary. Yesterday I grumbled about Mück, expecting him to take over from me, and today he has been dismissed. And guess who will be teaching *Philosophische Propaedeutik* in the Octava. Yes!!! I am delighted. It will mean a lot of work, but I know it will be rewarding. Not to mention what it does for my ego that I, the most junior among the staff, should be entrusted with it. It is a mix of psychology, logic, and history of philosophy – a tall order. I plan to pick out some "big" topic or question and work around it: art, beauty, goodness, free will, etc. They can have a choice – whatever they find relevant, since I intend to proceed through discussion. I may not be a Socrates, but I can look at his method. Who will hand me the poison? But seriously, I really am looking forward to it.

Burghardt is to take over my Tertia for Czech, but in return I get them for German. With my twenty-five hours a week in class, I have the biggest teaching load of everybody. But I don't mind. We had an uproar today in the Octava. I had informed them that as well as having me for Czech, as before, they would also be having me for philosophy, and that Professor Erna Menta would take over their Latin and German. Whereupon someone interjected, "That calls for a *dívčí válka*.[54] We object to having women in four subjects."

"Four subjects?" I said, "I am counting five." Eyes, ears, noses – gaping abysses of curiosity. "I thought you already knew that with Dr Bergmann gone, you would have Frau Burghardt, the other gym teacher."

You should have heard the hullabaloo. All hell broke loose. They shouted, threw up arms and legs; Switzinsky twirled around in his chair, the usually quiet Joksch got hold of Wiesner and shook him with excitement, and Hausner jumped on his desk. Later, in recess, they organized a mock demonstration, lit a candle, and prepared posters: "We will not play eurythmic volleyball" … "We'll refuse to undress," etc. They had a field day. To appreciate their reaction fully, one has to remember what a he-man's subject phys. ed. is and what a frilly type of woman Frau Burghardt is. She hadn't even been able to establish an appropriate relationship with the girls, whose gym teacher she had been up to now.

Not much time to think of myself or any personal problems, since every minute is taken up with preparation for classes. Just as well. And "my" class, the Prima, now has fifty students! It looks as if our school will survive at least to the end of the school year.

SATURDAY, 22 OCTOBER

Erna and I just returned from a movie. A silly little comedy with Moser, Lingen, etc. But we had a good laugh. Afterwards we continued talking and laughing, still in our seats, two absent-minded professors who didn't seem to have noticed that the show had finished – until suddenly we realized that we were there all alone. As we came out of the theatre, giggling about our absent-mindedness, we were respectfully greeted by two of our students, who stood at attention, clicking their heels, while at the same time two Czech soldiers gave us some wolf whistles from the other direction. A funny scene – or perhaps it only seemed so to me, like a continuation of the show we'd just seen, because I was ready for a liberating laugh.

Letter from Mutti. Papa has still not found work. And Mimi, who has been working as a governess, announced that she is giving up her job. Papa sounds annoyed with her, calls her irresponsible. Very unlike him. But everyone's nerves are wearing thin. And they obviously have reason to be worried.

Where are you? I am waiting from one mail to the next. The silence is deafening.

SUNDAY, 23 OCTOBER

Early, still in bed. Mulling over plans for my philosophy class got me thinking about all sorts of things that we take for granted. Not thinking really, just having random thoughts. About such "minor" details as the secret of organic life, the mystery of the mind ... How does the spark of intelligence originate? There is a hand that I can open and close at will. Chemists, physiologists, and doctors know precisely what bones and muscles consist of, but what about the human will that makes them move? Not to mention the grey matter that is the site of our minds. Where does the body end and the mind begin? Or look at a stone in contrast to a plant. What is the crucial step between the inert and the living, not so much in defining it, but in its happening?

Man has accomplished so much, but he cannot create life (apart from his own procreation). Yet he can take it. And once the thread of life breaks, it's over. We can kill far too easily. And think of that miraculous process by which living creatures procreate. Think of the huge tree that grew from a seed, or the human being that developed from a single cell. For me, it always comes back to this, that to take life is the ultimate evil.

MONDAY, 24 OCTOBER

Gotschlich returned today. That means that one of us will be redundant. I learned yesterday that they are starting to make files of all teachers who are members of the Henlein party and that in future only they will be allowed to teach in German schools in Czechoslovakia. This was supposedly Lachnit's idea.

I feel the noose tightening. Lachnit has been avoiding me. It seems only yesterday that he reassured me, "We take, after all, into account what person we are dealing with." There is new talk of Olmütz becoming part of the Reich. I don't care any longer. If only I had mail, from you or Mali. Rumour has it that mountains of undelivered mail are piling up at the post office.

But now something pleasant. I had my first German class in the Tertia, and they jumped and cheered when I came in. When I asked the Octava how far they had got under Mück, they broke into derisive laughter.

I am to join Erna today at her place to listen to an address by Baldur von Schirach about the "new youth" and their attitude to art!

2

Czechoslovakia

26 October 1938 – 20 February 1939

WEDNESDAY, 26 OCTOBER [1938]

Principal Lachnit informed me today that he had to declare me redundant. The official expression was *zur Verfügung stellen* – to be placed at the ministry's disposal. Until the ministry disposes otherwise, I shall continue to draw my salary and have some teaching duties. I asked him to leave me the philosophy class. Had my first session with them today. Afterwards, outside, I overheard Beigel say to the rest of them, "That was something else!" Later, when I had them for Czech, they pleaded, "Please, let's continue with philosophy instead." That was not possible, of course. But I was pleased.

Schenk returned today.

A sweet letter from Mimi. She too is learning English.

Later. Erna and I went for our walk as usual. We also did some shopping and also, as usual, lingered in various places for a chat and a review of the latest rumours. Call it gossip. We were talking to the baker when he called out, "Watch out, there come some Jews!" Erna was convulsed with laughter. I did not think it all that funny.

THURSDAY, 27 OCTOBER

The school received a request today to report the number of its Jewish students and teachers. (I am the only Jewish member of staff.) I also learned from Lachnit that it is official now that Jewish teachers are no longer to be employed at German-speaking schools. He thought I would probably be dismissed altogether. Despite the fact that I had seen it coming, I was very depressed.

On my way downstairs with Erna, I was called away by Mück, who wanted a word with me in private. He had been talking to Bergmann about me, and they had decided to do everything in their power to see that "not a hair on my head would be harmed." In his words, "dass mir kein Haar gekrümmt werde." They felt that now was the time to step in. What they had in mind was to get me a job at a Jewish school in Germany as a Czechoslovak citizen. They felt in this way I would be safe. If I made an application, they said, they would pass it on to the proper authorities in Berlin.

Bittersweet experiences in school today. The youngsters in the Prima were so lovable. It was sad to say goodbye. And when I told the Tertia that I would no longer be teaching them German, they formed a circle around me and declared they would let me out only if I promise that I would try to keep them. And so it went in every classroom.

FRIDAY, 28 OCTOBER

The boys of the Octava had to stay two hours after school because they had locked Burghardt in the gym earlier today. Dr Just was supposed to act as their jailer, but they asked if they could perhaps have a philosophy class instead. This was granted. And would you believe that the girls, who were not involved in the punishment, joined us for the two-hour session? They – the boys and girls – wanted to talk about all sorts of lofty subjects: good and evil, freedom of will, art and kitsch. The two hours went by in no time. When it was over, Havelka and Nawarre announced that they would have to lock Burghardt in again.

Speaking of good and evil, forgive the nonsense I wrote last summer, dear diary, when I was reading Oscar Wilde. Seems to me now that my concept of good was far too rigid. What is goodness? There are so many possibilities of doing or not doing good, kind, decent, appropriate things. But as Fontane says, "Das ist ein weites Feld, Luise!"[1] I just wanted to let you know that I have been thinking about it quite a lot lately, prompted by my discussions with the young people.

Had a walk with Erna this afternoon and then accompanied her to the station. She was going to Sternberg, where the Henlein party's headquarters for this area are now located. She took my letter along. Perhaps I'd better explain why I am trying to emigrate to Germany if I can. It seems like a joke. And it would be an even greater joke if, out of all my German colleagues who want to move there, I became the first to get a job in Hitler's Reich! There seems no chance at the moment of getting to England. Here in Olmütz I am "wafting in the breeze," so to speak, without any hope of another teaching job. But once I get firm employment with my Czech passport, I may be in a better position to move on to a position abroad. Do I make sense? Or am I merely proving that I am desperate enough to clutch at straws?

MONDAY, 31 OCTOBER

Mutti writes that they are trying to emigrate to Canada as farmers. That would be wonderful! Otto Proksch was here to say goodbye. He is moving to Germany to enlist in the Wehrmacht.[2] Erna reports that Baier has been moved to Berlin. She gave my letter to his daughter to be passed on.

Was able to deposit some money again. I had depleted my account when I bought the diamond. I now have 3,530 crowns in my account. The passage to Canada costs 3,400.

FRIDAY, 4 NOVEMBER

Rozehnal came back today. Brought me greetings from Bergmann, who sends word that he is about to travel to Berlin and will speak on my behalf.

Have typed "Walther" on the office typewriter at school. Will make a package and send it on. Wouldn't it be fun to meet a certain blond topknot somewhere in Berlin? Is that at the bottom of my crazy pipedream?

SUNDAY, 6 NOVEMBER

Have been lying awake half the night. The parents do not want to leave me here. I am to go with them to Canada. What would you advise me to do? If only we could talk! I have never felt more alone. I have been looking at our writing paper: the ladybugs, the double heart, the thirteen, the little angel, and, finally, the hiking boot. Yes, we have toyed with the idea for a long time, but it is turning into bitter fact. I must not allow myself to lose heart.

Autumn. The last yellow leaves are tumbling about in the air, and a damp, reddish-brown carpet covers the ground. With each breath you take in a whiff of decaying life.

Later. It's raining now. I have made a fire and am about to write a letter to Bergmann to thank him for his kindness. Wohlfahrtstädter will take it along to Neustadt.

MONDAY, 7 NOVEMBER

Three classes of Czech students have been moved into our school.

I don't know what is the matter with Erna. Yesterday she didn't call for me, and today she was very abrupt and disappeared at noon without making any arrangements for the afternoon as we usually do.

TUESDAY, 8 NOVEMBER

Have been trying to read *Mein Kampf* but didn't get very far. I find it rather overwhelming. No wonder Germans get swelled heads when reading it and consider themselves very lucky to be living in the Hitler era.

SATURDAY, 12 NOVEMBER

It has been a bad week. Night after night I buried myself in the pillows as if I could smother all thoughts and feelings, for there seemed no way out. I felt alone and desperate. Have been rereading Rilke's *Geschichten vom lieben Gott* [Stories of Our Dear Lord]. Remember how we used to read the stories together? And how you said that I would understand them better later in life? Well, I think I do now. Especially the last one, "Dem Dunkel erzählt" [Told to the Dark]. I am also rereading Rilke's *Stundenbuch* [The Book of Hours]. No, not rereading, but caressing the lines we savoured together and literally singing certain poems that you made into songs. Some I only understand now.[3]

SUNDAY, 13 NOVEMBER

Today is the thirteenth! And Sunday to boot. Stayed in bed until eleven, then rewrote the last scenes of "Walther." Went to school to ask Lachnit if I could use the office typewriter, and have now finished. All I have left to do is embroider a bookmark. I feel much better and am beginning to believe again in the possibility of a future, some future, for us. Did you know that there are German schools abroad for which teachers are continually being sought?

New anti-Jewish edicts have come out in Germany. So awful and mean that I cannot bring myself even to list them. Jews are being condemned to starve and die. Will that at last rouse the world? But the more injustice Germany commits, the more firmly I believe in our joint future: every new horror story makes it more likely that you will be able to leave with a clear conscience, without a feeling of ambivalence.

Have been walking with Erna for two hours, along the river and far into the country. This is the first time she has spoken of the German terror with bitterness and apparent horror. She is appalled at the happenings of Kristallnacht.[4] But she blames it all on a few hoodlums, believing that Hitler would not condone this sort of thing. Until now she had seemed blind.

With the exception of Erna, most teachers are beginning to avoid me. Evidently afraid. What a fool I was to consider moving to Germany! Had a letter from Mimi in which she scolds me and calls me crazy – and she is right.

MONDAY, 14 NOVEMBER

Letter from Bergmann, via Zapletal. (My fellow teachers seem like yoyos, travelling to the German-occupied area and back again while Olmütz itself is still under Czechoslovak jurisdiction.) Interesting and rather pathetic. He sympathizes with my difficult situation but regrets that he cannot help me, adding, "I myself have sunk into insignificance. In the days of need, my involvement and my sacrifice were welcomed, but now that we have achieved almost everything, there are enough people on hand. And so I live in the wood and wait."

TUESDAY, 15 NOVEMBER

All sorts of developments at school. The Sexta and Septima have sent a delegation to the principal with their collective demands: Hitler's picture to be hung in the classrooms instead of President Masaryk's; the raised arm and "Heil Hitler" salute to be permitted; to be allowed to adorn themselves with swastikas. In addition, the Sexta organized a *Sonderaktion* [special action], declaring that they would not enter the classroom as long as it contained a Jew. Wohlfahrtstädter didn't know how to deal with the situation and called for reinforcements against these sixteen-year-old youngsters. Lachnit arrived and promptly established order. What a mean, stupid, brutal, and vulgar world! How quickly the baser instincts take over! Equally if not more worrisome, how quickly Jews can be turned into outcasts. In the face of this treatment, is it possible to keep one's self-respect?

WEDNESDAY, 16 NOVEMBER

What do I tell first? That the latest rumour has Olmütz joining the Reich after all? Or that Burghardt has departed, apparently for good, and I have taken over phys. ed. in six classes (girls only)? Or that the principal had word from Brünn today that the teachers who had been "put at the ministry's disposal" are to continue with their former teaching assignments for the time being, but must not be officially included in future plans? Or that Freising reappeared today? Or that in reply to yesterday's "demands," the students were handed an official reprimand? Or that the whole town is plastered with posters of the Gajda party,[5] and people crowd in front of them open-mouthed? Or that over the last few days, Masaryk's picture has mysteriously disappeared from its usual places in the classrooms, leaving tell-tale clean areas on the wall? In one class, the president still overlooks proceedings, but Christ has been removed. (Did someone confuse them?) Today, a terse edict was issued ordering the presidential likenesses to be rehung without delay. But no one knows their whereabouts, and both janitors are frantically looking for them.

THURSDAY, 17 NOVEMBER

Erna tried to break it to me tactfully that she cannot reconcile it with her conscience to have a Jewess as her best friend. There has been no change, she assured me, in her feelings towards me. Nor has it anything to do with being afraid or saving face. For that, she said, it was too late. It was strictly a matter of conscience, of being consistent.

Now I am alone in every sense – not only inside but externally. No more half-measures. I am no longer the exception to whom all those nasty things they say about the Jews don't apply. Now that my last and only friend has cut me off, I am consumed by an almost morbid curiosity. What is going to happen next? I am going to the coffee house to find out. Have not been there for some time because it felt better being alone. Today, when I am alone not of my own choice, I want to go out. Will people speak to me? My turn has come now, and it is perhaps good that it has. It has been a shock and I will need some time to digest it.

So will Erna. After announcing that this must be the end of our friendship, she continued to talk about trivia. Does she think we can behave like a married couple that seeks to continue some civilized relationship after the divorce? That I shall be available whenever she wishes to talk to me but have not the right to claim her attention when I feel like it? I have too much pride for that. The break will have to be complete.

Oh dear diary, this has been a great shock. It also means a new daily routine. Eating lunch by myself. No more walks and discussions of anything and everything. Above all, a change not from choice or external necessity but because I am considered an outcast.

This is how Erna put it: "I have to discuss something with you of concern to us both. It was no accident that I haven't been with you the last two days. I have thought about it long and hard, but I cannot reconcile it with my *Weltanschauung* [ideology] to have a Jewess as my closest friend. Until now, I have looked on you as an exception, but now the moment of decision has come. This is no time for sentimentality.

Perhaps the situation will change. In the meantime, my personal feelings towards you remain the same as ever" … etc., etc. I said nothing.
What could I have said? Did she know how much it hurt?

Goodbye, Erna. It was a beautiful friendship. And now it's over, just
like that. It would have hurt less if you had kept away from me because
you were afraid, like the others. Only three days ago you were quite in-
dignant because Burghardt was obviously avoiding me. "She is smart," I
said, and you countered, "Not smart, only mean." How self-righteous
you are, you with your "good" motivation!

An amusing letter from Mimi arrived today. Thank goodness that life
goes on.

FRIDAY, 18 NOVEMBER

I spent a sleepless night and used up several handkerchiefs with my
tears. It is, after all, harder than I thought, without a change in external
circumstances and without personal reasons, simply to liquidate a
friendship. Easy for Erna, of course. For her, all kinds of doors are open.
For me, it was the last contact − the last real contact − with the world
around me.

SATURDAY, 19 NOVEMBER

A letter from Hella, good, loyal, dear Hella! It felt like a holiday. Yesterday
I called on Gerta Kassal in the hospital.[6]

Every evening, just before bedtime, I read one of Rilke's stories from
Geschichten vom lieben Gott. They seem to have been written especially
for me. Sent off letters to Hella and Sylvia Segerfelt[7] to ask Sylvia for
possible contacts in Sweden.

A conversation with Erna today as if nothing had changed. This is
how it came about. I was in the staffroom by myself when she came in
and told me, right away, that she was not feeling well. Appendix. Of
course I was sympathetic. Whereupon she asked whether I had seen the
Disney film. She had seen it yesterday and wants to see it again. Would I
go with her? I looked at her in surprise without saying anything. That
was the end of that. Later, there was some small talk. What does it

mean? Is she regretting her decision to cut me out of her life? But I am not a mouse to be played with. It won't do that I am at her disposal when she feels like it – for example, to go to the movies with her – but that I should never dare to suggest it myself. Of course the incident is trivial, but it is indicative of the one-sided relationship that is about to develop unless I clear the air. Does she think she is letting me down gently?

Trouble for Mück. He was transferred to Brünn two weeks ago. Rumour has it that he had a relationship with a student in the Octava. Now Principal Lachnit has reported him. Why now, after he was moved?

A package from home, full of goodies. Couldn't get the fire going in the stove, so I crawled into bed, shivering with cold.

WEDNESDAY, 23 NOVEMBER

Wanted to see Disney's *Snow White and the Seven Dwarfs*, but the queue was so long that I could only get tickets for today. I am looking forward to it. Do you remember? It was Christmas time, Vienna 1937, and snow was coming down in big, soft flakes, and two figures were tramping through the snow like two Santas. They had bought some goodies – ham, and cognac for the punch – before going into the cinema and allowing themselves to be carried off to Disney's wonderland. Afterwards, huddled together, they found the scene outside almost like a continuation of the fantasy they had just left and were startled by the hooting of each passing car. Contentedly, happily trotting home. Where is home now? When I couldn't get into the Disney movie yesterday, I comforted myself with a French film, *Prison without Bars*.

Young Altar[8] called on me with a Zionist paper and stayed about an hour. He tries very hard to make a Zionist out of me. Perhaps I could be an enthusiastic supporter of their cause if it were not for HF. It is like a curse, this inability to belong, because I am not wanted in the place where I felt at home (at least where I did feel at home until Hitler put an end to it), yet I'm not able to say yes without reservation to the Czechs or to the Jews. Altar invited me to a rehearsal of some spoken choral pieces that he is conducting.

Later. I went. It was a meeting of Zionist young people, who sang songs and spoke *Sprechchoere* [oral pieces]. How fortunate that these youngsters have this vision of a home in Palestine! Perhaps the only possible solution of the Jewish problem is to have a home where they can belong and can contribute and are accepted. But as I sat there, incognito as it were, among a dozen or so teenagers (aged about fifteen or sixteen) and listened to their melancholy, melodious songs, I felt like a stranger. The songs were beautiful but seemed foreign. I felt no bond, had no desire to join in. How would I have felt, I wonder, had I not known that this was a world you could never join and would not wish to?

On the way home – Altar was most chivalrous and accompanied his guest home – he bitterly complained about Erna, how her German lessons are turning into anti-Semitic tirades. Today's was a very painful experience for him, very depressing. How can the righteous Erna Menta be so mean? This morning in school she greeted me as if nothing had happened and asked if I had news from home. What am I to believe?

Tomorrow we go to see *Snow White*. You are coming with me, aren't you? I'll smuggle you in, no one will notice.

THURSDAY, 24 NOVEMBER

It's fabulous, magical. I am still quite numb. If you saw it – and I hope you will – you would go straight to Walt Disney and offer to work with him. And I could join you. Or another version of the dream, as I continued it: I am standing in a big office, talking to Walt. And one day soon afterwards someone in old Europe gets a letter from America with an invitation … Now I am not scared of America any longer. I should like to be in a world where they create things like that. It's so wonderful how everything in this film comes to life. The trees, the stones, the animals. Disney seems to love all things, all "ordinary" everyday things that we normally don't notice – almost like Rilke, except that his love is fresh and cheerful and full of fun. You leave the movie feeling that you are seeing everything with new eyes.

I have reorganized my days now that Erna is no longer part of my life. At noon I plan to go walking for an hour. Today I crossed the village of

Powel, following a street until it became a country road and then a path and finally a series of mud puddles and fields. Then I turned round and did the same in the other direction, until I was almost bogged down in a soggy ploughed field. It was beautiful, and I brought a lot of fresh air home with me, literally and figuratively.

SUNDAY, 27 NOVEMBER

Three letters, all from Mutti. I am to send applications to Makabi in Prague and include a photo; also to complete a questionnaire for Wizo, with two photographs.[9] Further, I am to send an English application to Woburn House, London. All in connection with some job in England. As well, I received an announcement of an opening to teach in South Australia. If only I could discuss it all with you! Australia seems too far away, so I am not following it up. Had my picture taken and gave them a friendly smile. Then I wrote the applications. Spoke to Altar to inquire about Makabi. He offered to write to them in support of my application.

Spent some time in the staffroom and had a chat with Principal Lachnit. He was very friendly and advised me not to do anything hasty. Easy for him to say! I wonder how many others have endured as much talk about the "Jewish plague" as I have. (They mean it as a compliment, suggesting that I am the exception, the acceptable good Jew ...) No, I have had it here.

Bergmann is to return here. "The old man" asked for him. I picked up my pictures. The photographer's daughter is a pretty young blonde. Today she asked, "Do you have many friends?" "None," I replied. Whereupon Miss Waldek said, "That encourages me. I wanted to ask you yesterday whether you would come and visit us sometime." To make it short, we'll meet tonight in the coffee house. She is half-Jewish – looks like three Aryans rolled into one. Strange how new doors open unexpectedly.

TUESDAY, 29 NOVEMBER

Sat and talked with Hansi Waldek in the coffee house until 11:30 PM. Of course I learned her life story. She had been engaged to a German who has simply disappeared from her life. Now she is in love with a Jew, but his parents are orthodox and would never allow him to marry a half-Christian. Did I tell you the story of Dr Losova, whom I tutored in German? She too had one great love in her life, an orthodox Jew who couldn't marry her. Ring around the roses ...

Later. When I entered the Octava yesterday, the lamps were once again swinging. Perhaps I haven't mentioned this before. Our classrooms are lit by several lamps that are suspended from the ceiling, dangling by metre-long cords. The temptation to set them swinging – preferably in different directions – seems irresistible. Normally I might just have laughed. But today I had prepared a serious lecture and was looking forward to a rousing discussion. Stepping into this monkey cage, I couldn't imagine how I could talk philosophy in this atmosphere. But I swallowed my disappointment and anger, and without comment pulled out the book in which I enter grades and then started to examine the class on the material they were supposed to have prepared. When the lamps stopped swinging I began to lecture. It really was a good talk. You could have heard a pin drop.

On my way home, Altar caught up with me. "That was great how you ignored the lamps! As if you didn't notice." And he proceeded to tell me how they did it with all their teachers as a test of sorts, to compare reactions. Professor Schenk had become very excited – an enormously satisfying success. "You passed the test by far the best. Simply super!"

Those scoundrels! It was lucky I didn't explode. And the reason I didn't? Because for once I really minded.

THURSDAY, 1 DECEMBER

What a streak of good luck! I'll start with the best. Today, Erna said, "There's something on the radio tomorrow that will interest you. If you wish, you can listen at my place." (I have no radio, which also means that I am not informed about programming.)[10] Great! But what do I do about the staff meeting that has been called for the same hour? What excuse do I find to give Lachnit? Second stroke of luck. Out of the blue, the principal postponed the meeting to Monday. (Where will you be listening to the program? In Komotau? In Vienna?)

More nice things: A very warm letter from Maña from Brussels. Also one from Hella.[11]

There is more. The principal telephoned Brünn and was told that I would be "made available" (that is to say, transferred) to the Bohemian Department of Education. In Bohemia, the only remaining institutions are in Prague and Pilsen, which means that I will be near either the parents or Uncle Charles. I was going to send all my things to the parents at Christmas anyway. Now perhaps I'll have the transfer paid for. Meanwhile, I am continuing to teach here: all the girls' gym classes, plus philosophy (Octava). From next Monday, no more Czech classes will be offered.

When I entered the Tertia today, they greeted me with arms raised in a "Heil Hitler," and above my desk was his picture, flanked by swastikas. I said, "You know that this is not allowed. Do you want the Czech janitor to take it down? Wouldn't it be better if you did it yourselves? You can still picture it there in your mind, if that is what you want." Or something like that. Whereupon several came forward, took down the flags, and made Hitler face the wall so that he now looks like an innocent calendar. I hope his nose is being squashed. Was asked to substitute in the Septima. I went in with some trepidation – they are known as the most rabid lot. To my surprise, they applauded wildly when I entered. How come? You figure it out, diary.

Last night I went to a movie with Hansi Waldek and her mother. A Viennese film: *Hannele and Her Lovers*. Utter kitsch. The Waldeks invited me to their place for this afternoon. I'll go there a little later.

One piece of not so pleasant news. The Kassals will be moving in ten days.

FRIDAY, 2 DECEMBER
What a disappointment! The broadcast was cancelled or pre-empted. Already for the fourth time. I can imagine how sad you must be.

The Führer is to speak tonight. Herr Kundt, a Sudeten German member of the Czechoslovak parliament, was in Olmütz yesterday.[12] His message: For the time being, nobody needs to decide whether to opt for the Czech or German side; the Führer wants to come to Prague. (Translation: There won't be a Czechoslovakia anyway.) The decision will be made before Christmas.

Meanwhile, our school is already under Berlin jurisdiction: there was a letter from the Education Department in Brünn confirming that the school has been placed under Berlin authority. Jewish teachers are to be dismissed.

MONDAY, 5 DECEMBER

Letters from Mrs Auerbach and Hans Pollak.[13] Once again, I have to force myself to start from the beginning. I had written several letters: to Mrs Auerbach for a reference, to Mrs Rüdinger with regard to the teaching post in Australia for which I am not applying, to Mutti, and to Maña. Received a reply from London. The only jobs available are for domestics who can cook.

TUESDAY, 6 DECEMBER

Hansi Waldek came (unexpectedly) to pick me up for supper. From now on, I am to cook at their place (to train me). I started right away.

Before yesterday's staff meeting, the principal called me into his holiest of holies. He wanted to notify me privately that, as of 1 January, no Jewish teachers will be allowed to teach. Gave my first gym class yesterday.

My dear diary. You are my only friend now. I feel lonely and miserable.

SATURDAY, 10 DECEMBER

Every morning throughout this week I have cooked with Mrs Waldek. She is a kind, pleasant, bright person, an excellent cook, and a good and patient instructor. In the afternoon I usually typed stuff for the principal. Since my teaching duties are so limited, he uses me as his office help. Good practice too.

Spent two evenings with the Waldeks as well. On one occasion, in the coffee house with Hansi, we were joined by a woman who introduced herself to me as a member of Wizo [a Jewish women's organization] and asked me to come to their office on Monday. They want to give me the address of their London headquarters and some appropriate references so that I can get a "congenial" position. I wonder who my guardian angel was in this instance. Which of my students? Altar also mentioned that a Dr Tauber, who is said to be a high mogul in various local Jewish organizations, wishes to get in touch with me to explore where he can be of help.

In yesterday's meeting Lachnit welcomed us with the Hitler salute. From that moment on, it has been *the* form of greeting in the staffroom, replacing the handshake.

Last night I had a nightmare: I dreamed that you and I went for a walk together, on the street, in broad daylight. Frau Kassal told me this morning that her husband is driving to Vienna today. How I would have liked to go along! I thought about it a long time.

Today I start packing my belongings. Will you follow me out of the country, as you said you would? Will you find a way? Where are you now? With your family? Bent over your desk? Sitting at the piano? Standing in a concert hall or theatre? I no longer know where to reach you with my thoughts – or where to address a letter if I dared to write you. And from now on, you don't have an address for me either.

FRIDAY, 16 DECEMBER

I am twenty-five years old today. For the first time in nine years, I celebrate this day without you. Letter from Mimi. After some very sweet preliminaries, noting that I am concluding my first quarter-century, she wishes me the fulfilment of all my wishes – that is to say, speedy emigration along with a wonderful professorial position.

Mutti also writes in her loving way. My present is a housecoat, which Gerti will make when I get home. She passes on wishes from Papa, who had to get up at 4:30 AM to take the train to Beroun for some negotiations on behalf of Aunt Milly. He has been going back and forth to Prague, together with Děda Steiner,[14] and they have almost daily telephone conversations with Brussels to settle affairs for Uncle Louis, who apparently left a great mess behind.

Aunt Milly had additional problems. Someone sent word that she should come back to Komotau to discuss the sale of her house with an interested buyer. But other reports said that her furniture had all been smashed. And now someone has called, with a message from an anonymous friend, to warn her not to return to Komotau in any circumstances. The previous message seems to have been a trap. Why would anyone want to harm Aunt Milly? Because the family was considered fairly wealthy? Or because they recently had Czech-speaking tenants in their house? Scary!

Mutti also reports that they have a boarder in Kralupy, a Mr Strassberg from Bärringen. His wife, an Aryan, had to remain there: "He lives in our tiny spare room. A clean, little old man (sixty-four), rather lonely and pitiful." They are all trying to learn English. Mutti does it with gusto, but Papa finds it hard. I am not surprised. Robert and Bertl Steiner[15] are helping them. They also want to emigrate. Perhaps to Australia.

One of Mimi's darling letters. First of all she gives me hell for thinking of moving to Germany when others would do anything to get out: "Don't you read the papers? Don't you know what is going on?" Of course I do. And of course I know. And of course she is right. Further: "We are preparing for Canada. I am learning to make butter. It is not as easy as it might seem, but I'll get there yet, given enough time and practice. Last night we divided our work. Mutti is to do the cooking and to feed and supervise (sic!) the poultry. Papa will work on the field(s), and I shall drive the tractor. Don't worry, we'll find something for you to do when the time comes, so you won't feel useless." Papa, she says, is learning farming on the estate of a certain Mr Sablin: "During the first lesson they found out that they have mutual acquaintances and gave them a thorough going over. I am curious what else Papa is going to learn there."

About her present job with the Singer family, Mimi reports: "I have lots of fun with the children. Usually without their knowing it. The other day, for instance, when the little one spat at her brother and I had to punish her, I gave her a choice: either a sound spanking from me or her word of honour never to spit on anyone again. She considered it at length and then inquired, 'What does word of honour mean? How long does it last? Does it apply just to brother Mirko or does it include my friend next door as well? How sound would my spanking be?' Eventually, she opted for the word of honour."

As for myself, when I am not teaching I spend my mornings with the Waldeks, cooking under Mrs W's supervision. My room here is terribly cold. I still spend the afternoons here, mostly writing applications: to Wizo Prague, to Alliance Française (suggested by Mrs Auerbach), to a Czechoslovak Refugee Committee in London, to Maňa, asking her to place an ad in the *Daily Telegraph* for me. I could not present myself at the local Wizo on Monday because I had classes. Tuesday, a Jewish student brought me a message: I am to go to Mrs Ing. Gross, who is president of the local branch of Wizo, and bring a curriculum vitae. They had discussed what could be done for me and wondered whether I could teach in a refugee camp.

SATURDAY, 17 DECEMBER

Express letter from Mutti. If only Hella would come so that I can give her a message for Hans before leaving here for good!

Later. Letter from Hella. She is coming tomorrow! As if decreed by fate. So of course I shall postpone my departure.

SUNDAY, 18 DECEMBER

A quaint letter from Sylvia,[16] who will make inquiries on my behalf in Sweden. Also a nice letter from Maňa, who put an ad in the *Daily Telegraph* for me. And last but not least, a message from Hella. She did not get an *Uebertrittschein* [permission to cross the border].

MONDAY, 19 DECEMBER

Last day in Olmütz. I was in a quandary. Should I say goodbye to Erna? In the end I did. After all, our close friendship of last year was real and cannot be wiped out. She said she might travel to Vienna, in which case she would inquire after your whereabouts. Later this afternoon I shall pay a last visit to the Waldeks. And I happened to run into Altar on the street. He is quitting school (how much longer would he have been allowed to attend?) and plans to leave for England, hoping to get into a camp in preparation for emigration to Palestine.

WEDNESDAY, 21 DECEMBER

In Kralupy. I am already in bed, having just luxuriated in a bath. The apartment Louis and Maña left us is fabulous – at least it seems so to us.

The trip was strenuous, what with all my luggage and having to change stations in Prague. Fortunately, there was always some gentleman's strong arm ready to give help when it was most needed. Would I get as much help if I were old and wrinkled?

Mutti is not feeling well. She thinks that her tumour is acting up again. And, diary, you'll find it hard to believe this, but she wrote to her doctor in Komotau (who has treated her for many years), asking for a copy of his file or a report on her treatment, and she received no reply.

I shall pitch in and help to give her a chance to rest. We had a long talk today. Mutti really is a very courageous person. Strange, she always seemed so full of fears and anxieties, but now that it comes to the crunch, she is a tower of strength. Only once did she break down and weep – when she asked after HF and I had nothing to say. She has always been very fond of him. *I* had to comfort *her*. "I miss him so much," is how she put it.

TUESDAY, 27 DECEMBER

I have been too busy to report. Busy with ordinary daily chores. Come to think of it, for the first time in my life. I am the first to get up in the morning. I start the fire, make coffee, tidy the kitchen before the others come. Then, after breakfast, I do the dishes, either with Mutti or by myself, go shopping, and cook. Then dishes again. In Komotau, a maid always handled these "details." I am actually enjoying it, but the day is gone before I know it.

This is the first time I have been alone at home since I arrived a week ago. Except, of course, when I'm in bed. Every evening, before going to sleep, I daydream about the future. Castles in Spain. I actually dared write you a letter last Sunday – a real letter, not just one in my head or to this diary. Has it reached you? Much of the time I feel so full of emotion – I have the feeling that it shows. Is that why everyone is so good to me?

Maña wants me to join her, and I have been to the Belgian consulate to apply for a visa. Will I get it? Maña is so good to me. She has always been wonderfully generous, even though I am not her blood relation. I was thinking back to that time I was invited to her parents' home the summer before they were married – that memorable summer – and there was the summer I spent with them in Grenoble. Not to forget Maña's magnificent, glamorous hand-me-downs, the three show-stopper rhinestone-studded gowns, the leopard fur, the snakeskin purse, the hand-embroidered pink kimono – treasures she might have saved for her daughter or given to some of her own relatives.

I wrote to Sylvia. To get to Sweden would of course be best of all – safe but not totally out of reach. I have also been to Prague in connection with Canada. Canadian women, it seems, are pressuring their government to permit some women refugee "intellectuals" to come in and work in their own professions. So a list of applicants is being prepared, and my name is on that list.

Yesterday we were in Pilsen. Cousin Lilly has arrived from Paris with husband Felix Munk and their baby Peter. She seems unchanged. Except, of course, for that eighteen-month-old tot babbling away in French. When she inquired after HF, I lied that we had separated in 1933.[17] She found that "sensible." Lilly has always been a pragmatist. We drove to Pilsen in the Pollaks' car, with cousin Hans Pollak as a chauffeur, and almost didn't make it. On the return journey, the car skidded on an icy patch on the highway, turning around 180 degrees so that we continued for some metres in the opposite direction – to the accompaniment of an *a cappella* chorus of panic-stricken passengers. A little while later, back in Prague, when we were still recovering from the narrow escape, Hans turned from Italska Street into Fochova without noticing the car that was approaching along Fochova. It bumped right into us. Nobody was hurt, nor was there serious damage except for some dents, but Papa had to fork over 150 crowns to the other driver. If it had been a bus or streetcar I would not be here to write a diary.

I almost forgot. It is now official. As of 1 January, Jewish teachers will not be allowed to teach in German schools in Czechoslovakia and are on indefinite leave. So there goes the profession for which I had prepared myself and to which I had looked forward. But there is no room for sentiment now.[18]

SUNDAY, 1 JANUARY [1939]

Our ninth anniversary. Did my Christmas message reach you? No need to tell you how lonely I feel or what my thoughts and wishes are. Is there any hope that we shall celebrate our tenth together?

SATURDAY, 7 JANUARY, MIDNIGHT

A letter from you arrived on 2 January!!! The mailman handed it to me as I was on my way to the station, to Voděradek, to visit Mimi. But for all my pleasure (and no need to describe it!) the letter contains something that I find puzzling, not to say disturbing. You mention corresponding with Erna. Why did she write to you? And if she did it for my sake, why did she not tell me about it? Will she tell me tomorrow? For, believe it or not, I have to return to Olmütz. A telegram arrived today: "Necessary to report for duty." In a way I am glad − mostly to have a chance of finding out what is going on between Erna and HF. What if she doesn't mention it? I am almost scared.

SUNDAY, 8 JANUARY

Back in Kralupy, 9:30 PM. Got up at 5 AM, dragged my suitcase to the station, and went to Prague. There I wrote an application for a job in England, helping to look after ten-month-old twins. I was aching all over and felt flu coming. So instead of taking the 2:30 train to Olmütz, I returned to Kralupy.

TUESDAY EVENING, 10 JANUARY, IN OLMÜTZ

Immediately after arrival (7 PM) I went to see Principal Lachnit. He was friendly as always. Wants me to continue teaching! Doesn't that amount to cruelty to animals? But I am not to start right away, not before he has discussed my status with the Department of Education in Brünn. He inquired about my plans, and I gave him a rather vague and general reply. (As if I could have said anything specific even had I tried!) He then gave me a little lecture on the pleasure and beauty of farming, leading up to the advice that no matter where I finally end up, I should marry a farmer.

I then went to see the Waldeks. Hansi was in bed with bad cramps. Poor thing, she gets them every month. Finally went home to my room, washed thoroughly, and wrote three English job applications.

I keep talking about myself. All this is boring compared with what's going on elsewhere. In Prague, for instance, Aunt Milly maintains an atmosphere of excitement and panic involving everyone around her. Ruth is giving her additional trouble – stays away for days and nights without saying where she has been. Remember your prophecy, the day Milly persuaded Mutti not to let us stay with the Pollaks in Priesen overnight? Aunt Antschi had invited us – after all of us had been in Tschachwitz together – and Mutti had given permission; but after listening to Aunt Milly, she came back from the station and made us return home with her. We were so disappointed. "Just you wait till her daughters grow up," you said.

Uruguay is the latest place on her agenda. If you can hand over 8000 crowns *today*, you can emigrate there. If only she were there already!

I can hardly wait to meet Erna tomorrow. What will she tell me?

WEDNESDAY, 11 JANUARY

Erna was mum. She asked me if I had heard from you and I shook my head. How can I trust her? Yet I cannot believe that she is mean. Hard and ruthless, yes, especially where her "principles" are concerned. What am I to believe? I am groping in vain for an explanation. We had a lengthy conversation. She was surprised that I had come back. "What is the point?" she asked. "In two weeks they will dismiss you anyway. Why don't you report sick? Your nerves are more important." (Do I really look so poorly? I have my period and am feeling rotten, it is true.) But the one thing she could have told me to make me feel better was never said. I tried to encourage her by asking how she had spent Christmas. Had she heard from Hain? (Her former fiancé. He wouldn't marry her because he was a Westphalian and she was from another *Stamm* [tribe].)

She said, "I no longer yearn for the Reich. It is nothing but a chase after jobs. I am what I am anywhere."

What are you, Erna? To me, an enigma. I can't justify your treatment of me, yet I can't stop trusting you. In conversation with Mrs Schroepfer I mentioned Mutti's distress about not getting a reply from her family doctor of many years, and Schroepfer said, "Can't you appeal to his humanity?" Whereupon Erna laughed contemptuously as if to say, "The Germans and humanity!" How naive can you get! Tell me, what am I to think? Am I just stupid or weak (or strong?) because I'm not able to give up my faith in Erna's basic goodness? But why did she write if not to help me? And if so, why won't she tell me? It has been another serious jolt.[19]

"The old man" spoke with the inspector. I have already been assigned to the Czech Department of Education but am to wait here for the official decree. In the meantime, I am to work in the school office. Colleague Schroepfer – the male variety – is most helpful. Today he drafted two letters in English – to the British Ministry of Education and to a female university professor (an Indologist), whom he suggested I approach on spec. Who knows? Perhaps I'll strike it lucky.

Have invited Hella here. Perhaps she'll come on Saturday. I can hardly wait for the thirteenth! And that it should be the thirteenth of all days – your lucky day, ever since that first performance of your songs on 13 May 1934. Was this your choice, or was it fate? This time, let's hope that all will go well. My fingers are crossed so tightly that it hurts! I wonder if Erna will invite me to listen to her radio as she did last time. But Hanne, why don't you try and get Erna out of your mind?

Just for fun, here is the list of the places to which I have sent applications:

Woburn House, London
Czechoslovak Committee for Refugees, London
Makabi, London
Wizo, Prague
Wizo, Olmütz
Through Frau Ing. Gross, to London (?)
Alliance Française (through Frau Auerbach)
Women's League for Peace and Freedom, Canada
Daily Telegraph – ad
Telegraaf, Holland – ad
Sylvia Segerfelt, Sweden
Belgian Consulate for visa
Ladies' League, London
Three job applications to England
Reichsministerium, Berlin
United States Consulate
L. Robitschek concerning an affidavit
Board of Education, London
Mrs Rhys Davis, Chipstead, England
Die Tat, Prague
E.M. Kay, Domestic Employment Agency, Chesterfield, England

FRIDAY, 13 JANUARY, 2:30 AM

While typing for the principal yesterday, I suddenly felt feverish. I came home and crawled into bed (no energy to build a fire) feeling lousy: a high temperature, a nasty cough, heart pounding as if it wanted to jump out of my rib cage. All alone. Very miserable.

Later in the morning. Luckily my pen went dry during the night or this would have turned into a plaintive litany. I felt deserted and scared. I am a little better now. My main worry is whether I'll be able to get to a radio tonight. What rotten luck!

5:45 PM. Have been busy swallowing quinine to bring the fever down so that I can go to the Kassals to listen to their radio. Only a few more minutes.

6:30 PM. What a joy! Enough to fill many empty days! It was beautiful. How you have matured! I felt it as a personal greeting, a message. Didn't you tell me not long ago (was it really only last July?) that your Walther von der Vogelweide experience "lives and dies with me" and that the *Vogelweide Lieder* were written for me and always will be?

14 JANUARY 1939

Hella is coming today: my "Walther von der Vogelweide" radio script is about to be sent on its way.[20]

6:30 PM. What a day it has been! The morning was spent with preparations: along with the manuscript, a letter, of course. Since I am not supposed to go out yet, I asked Frau Kassal to get some mandarin oranges and cookies for my guest. And then I waited. Impatiently. Hella was due around 1:30. But it was 2 PM ... 2:15 ... and still no Hella. At last the doorbell went. But it was Altar, the loyal disciple. He was not admitted into the "inner sanctum" but was advised that the lady was not well. Could he come another day? Perhaps tomorrow?

At last, Hella! And an hour later, in walked Hedi Scharff, one of my girls from the Octava. She came to return a book. A Czech book which, frankly, I had totally forgotten about. She had gone to the Waldeks with it, and Hansi had sent her on here. She talked about school, stuff that was sweet to hear – how sorry they were not to have me any longer, how fond they had been of me, and that they preferred me to my successor (Erna, even though she teaches according to their taste – meaning that she is a solid German nationalist). I had to promise to come to class to say goodbye before I leave.

Yet another caller: Dr Losova. She is a dear. She looked in as my doctor and as a friend. Promised to come again tomorrow.

Had a good visit with Hella despite the interruptions. I poured my heart out and appointed her my executrix – with regard to my scanty literary remains at any rate! We had some good laughs. It seems that every other family is in trouble because so many grandmothers were born out of wedlock, which makes it very difficult to get the *Ariernachweis* [proof of Aryan purity], for which no less than fifty documents are required. Nowadays, to have an illegitimate child is much less trouble than to discover an illegitimate grandmother in one's family closet!

SUNDAY, 15 JANUARY

Just arrived: an acceptance from England, offering me the job of looking after the baby twins. I want to shout and sing, and jump for joy, but all I can do is sneeze and stay quietly under the covers. Hurrah! Hurrah! Hurrah! Now I shall soon be on my way.

I'd better catch you up on how it all came about. A week ago yesterday – that was Saturday – while still in Kralupy, I had a call from Heinz Blumberg, Gerti's fiancé, to say that Gerti[21] had a job offer from an agency to which she had applied through his, Heinz's, English cousin. But in the meantime she had accepted a job as a cook, so … etc., etc. Thus, on my way to Olmütz last Sunday, I stopped over in Prague for a few hours and we included my application, along with Heinz's letter to his cousin, in which he explained that Gerti etc., etc. I sent it off by airmail. And today, forwarded express from Kralupy, the reply is here. How fast the mail works! From Prague to London to Chesterfield to Kralupy to Olmütz – all from one Sunday to the next. It is comforting to know that the world is that small.

MONDAY, 16 JANUARY

No visitor all day yesterday. Not the doctor and not Hansi Waldek or Altar. I am surprised that Hansi hasn't looked in on me in the five days I have been laid up. When she was ill, I stayed with her every afternoon. And she doesn't know that I am not seriouly ill.

Altar came to visit me today, and this time he was invited in. Reported that he had met Erna on the street in Brünn during the Christmas holidays. She asked him for my address and whether he knew my plans. I can't figure her out. It's a mystery, the type you get in those kitschy romances. Is she one of the good guys or one of the bad guys? Instead of finding out at the end of the book, I'll probably never know. A novel has a beginning and an ending, but life isn't organized so neatly. It has a beginning and an end all right, but the main character doesn't know the ending.

Speaking of organization, if only I were better organized, I'd have licked my flu long ago. But one day I had a high fever, the next day I coughed, and on the next I sniffled and sneezed. Why couldn't I have been more efficient and done it all simultaneously? Today I am convalescing.

Later the same day. There was almost a party of Octavans in my room. Unplanned and spontaneous, of course, at least as far as I know. First to arrive was Herta Weiss, with a gorgeous pot of African violets. She was still here when Hansi Waldek appeared. And just as Hansi was leaving, Paula Skrezek turned up, followed by Hedi Scharff with a bag of sweets and Altar with an English book. Altar and Paula left in due course, but Hedi Scharff stayed and stayed and might still be here if the doctor hadn't arrived. Losova is a dear person – but I have already said that. Her warmth and concern really make me feel good. My fever is gone, but I still have some bronchitis and am supposed to stay in bed for two more days.

Losova has been on the lookout for a position for me (without any prompting from me, needless to say) and came up with the suggestion that I might do secretarial work (type Czech and German correspondence) for the lawyer Meier. If I had been going to stay here any length of time, I would have considered it. Her brother, who is also a lawyer, was the go-between. Very kind of them. She made me promise to write to them from England.

Herta Weiss asked for a photo. Of course I gave her one, and when I wrote on it "For my dear Herta, Hanne Fischl, January '39," she was as happy as if I had given her a big present. She is a dear, a perfect *Backfisch* [teenage girl; literally, a fried fish]. H. Waldek (I find it difficult to call her Hansi; that name is reserved) got quite a kick out of the fact that Herta, who is about a foot taller than I am and much bigger all round, is always so shy with me and greets me with *Küss die Hand* [a kiss on the hand]. My illness actually could not have come at a better time. I no longer have a job in Olmütz anyway. This way, I have simply been taken out of circulation temporarily, with people and things having to come to me instead of me chasing after them. It allows me time to prepare myself (internally) for my farewell to good old bad Europe. And isn't it nice that even though I have abdicated, some of my students are still pampering me!

Hella gave me the book *Frühling im Elbtal* [Springtime in the Elbe Valley] by Willy Lang. A kitschy romance, but it calls up so many memories that I can barely read on. Come to think of it, everything I look at and touch awakens memories. I guess I'm all churned up inside. Keep thinking of how we used to roam through the woods at this time of year and always had to rush home because we had stayed too long. Looking back, I regret having spoiled my enjoyment by being overanxious. Or sitting around the table in the evening, our hands sometimes secretely touching. And remember the first of January? I thought of it today, for the hundredth time, as a *fata morgana* [mirage].

WEDNESDAY, 18 JANUARY

Diary! A letter from America. Those relatives named Froeschl have written, promising affidavits for Mimi and me. (What kind of transformation can produce Froeschl out of Fischl? Are little frogs better than little fish? Will we too turn into frogs?) So, in about a year, it will be adieu to Europe for sure.

Also, the principal sent word that my decree has arrived, so I can leave as soon as I am well enough. I wrote to Hella immediately, enclosing a letter to be passed on to H. Then I had to compose an epistle in English to Mr Froeschl, Milwaukee, Wisconsin, on behalf of Mimi and myself. I am still in bed. Hope to be allowed up tomorrow.

Now that I have reported today's big news I can catch up with yesterday's little happenings. H. Waldek was here in the evening and asked about the book she found me reading. So I told her the story of *Frühling im Elbtal*. Springtime in the Elbe Valley – the name says it all. Young lovers are separated by a cruel fate, and he ends up in America. No sign of life from him, so everyone assumes he is dead. Everyone except his beloved Maria(!), who continues to wait for his return. After seventeen years of silence he returns, and they get married and live happily ever after. After hearing this tear-jerker plot, H.W. was quiet for a moment and then said, very seriously, "I think you would be capable of that too. I mean, of waiting seventeen years."

I was flabbergasted to hear her say that, for she knows nothing about me, about us. She is rather flirtatious herself and has been wondering (out loud) why I don't seem interested in men. When I didn't reply, she figured it out this way – that I had a great love some time ago and we parted, and that after this disappointment I had refused to get involved. Since she herself gets involved rather easily and frequently (though, I gather, not beyond the kissing stage), she looks on me as a sort of saint.

This morning she sent me through a messenger (the Waldeks' apprentice) a little note, a book, and a clean nightie. The latter was especially welcome, since I had brought only one with me, thinking I was just coming for a day or so. And I have only the dress I was wearing when I arrived. Mutti inquires in a letter how I am managing with my wardrobe. As you see, I settled everything by getting sick.

THURSDAY, 19 JANUARY

Finally out of bed. I even ventured outside, but my knees wobbled so I quickly returned to my room.

A quiet day. In the morning, Altar, the faithful, came for his daily visit. And Herta just left. Why do these visits please me so? Remnants of professorial vanity? There can be no more questioning of students' motives – the time for apple polishing is over. (Quite the opposite, in fact, because it's now the time for shunning.) It renews one's faith in human decency. Herta invited me to have supper at their house tomorrow. It will be my last evening in Olmütz – if Hella comes during the day. I can't leave without seeing her first. She is our only link.

But in the meantime, there are still some errands, mostly farewell visits. The Waldeks, of course. And in school. Secretly – without even admitting it to myself – I had been hoping from day to day that Erna would show up. I think I would have gone to see her if I knew she was sick and alone. I feel like leaving without saying goodbye to her, but I'm afraid I won't be able to do that. One way or the other, I shall leave here with a sense of inner emptiness. Darn it, why can't I get my mind off Erna? I tell myself that I ought to hate her, but when she stands before me I can't believe that she is a bad person and I still have warm feelings for her.

<h3 style="text-align:center">FRIDAY, 20 JANUARY</h3>

I made my farewells at school. First I went to the Octava. It was their ("our") philosophy period. Now with Suchanek. As I entered, they all rose and remained standing. I said (more or less), "I have come to say goodbye, but I can't leave without telling you how much I have enjoyed working with you and how much I appreciated your honest cooperation." I wanted to say more but felt I was choking up, so I concluded rather quickly, "I hope that all of you will turn into good, fair, honest, and happy people. Goodbye" – and out I went before they could catch their breath. But I still see them before me: Schönwälder and his embarrassed grin, Herta's and Paula's sad eyes. You could have heard a pin drop.

Later, during recess, Annie Strauss – another student – came to the staffroom door to say goodbye in person. And then I was in the principal's office. He exuded genuine warmth and said over and over again how fond the students had been of me. And not to worry, "they" would surely soon establish Jewish schools. In the staffroom, instead of going round to say goodbye to everyone, I posted a note on the board, with warmest good wishes and a farewell to all my colleagues.

As for Erna, right in front of me, she began to let off steam about an objectionable Jewish girl in the Octava, adding, "There will have to be a great reckoning between Europe and that part of the world where Jews congregate" (meaning, of course, the United States). Perhaps I ought to have given her some advice: Just go around spreading your sort of opinion and then give the Jews a piece of land in which to live – as a bait and trap, so to speak – and if and when your war breaks out, you can make short shrift of them.[22]

Ressel added his bit to the conversation: "How can anyone expect the Sudeten Germans to forget the many bombers the Jews have contributed to the Czech state?" This was a reference to the response to the appeal for a Czechoslovak Defence Fund. I said nothing, of course. With a mere "goodbye" I left the room. That was my parting from Erna.

KRALUPY, 27 JANUARY

Here I am, surrounded by mountains of ironing. But it will have to wait. At last I am alone at home. Mutti just went out and I have a chance to catch up on a whole week of news without having to answer questions about what I'm up to.

The parting from Olmütz was very emotional. Did I mention my final conversation with the principal? As I was leaving, he kissed my hand, as if wanting to demonstrate his respect. Earlier, he had tried to comfort me by saying that he, too, may be cut off from his home (meaning Germany) for good. But I didn't let him get away with that. There is a world of difference, I reminded him, between having a respected position with one's family by one's side, albeit away from home, and not having a homeland anywhere or even a job, and having to leave one's family perhaps for good; and, what's more, being in a situation in which every street urchin with an *Ariernachweis* [Aryan certificate] thinks he has a right to spit on you. There was a long pause after that, the principal sitting very still.

On Friday afternoon Hella came from her home in Bärn for one last visit. After walking with her to the station, I went to the Weiss family for supper. On Saturday, a last visit with the Waldeks and Dr Losova, and on Sunday it was goodbye Olmütz for ever. A strange feeling that, knowing it really is the last time.

Papa had come to Prague to meet me. I arrived at Wilson Station at 11:35 AM and ran to the post office. Nothing there. Or at home. Now I am beginning to worry that mail may be going astray. The only thing waiting for me was a card from Mrs Rhys Davis, the university professor – Indologist – in London to whom I had written.

Yesterday I presented myself at the Department of Education in Prague. They said that I still belong to Brünn; my transfer has not yet arrived. I am to wait here. (I should hope so! I suppose they don't know what to do with me either. How could they?)

When will the permit for England arrive? Disquieting rumours of imminent war are making the rounds. If there is a war and I am in England, we would be in enemy camps. Horrible thought. There are also rumours that an "internal" revolution is brewing in Germany and that there will soon be a change for the better. I can't believe it. Based on nothing but wishful thinking, I am sure.

Mutti and I went to see a gynaecologist yesterday. Mutti, who has been worrying about her so-called tumour, was told that she is perfectly healthy. That's great news! And the gynaecologist told me that he hopes I will always stay as healthy as I am now.

Monday I am to travel to Prague to take a domestic exam for Wizo. To this end I am studying *Herrenhemdenbügeln* [ironing men's shirts]. Remember the mountain that is awaiting my attention? Just one more moment!

Mimi is to come home next Tuesday. She and Mutti and all the sundry cousins and aunts are to learn to make gloves. Uncle Louis is moving his glove factory to Canada and has promised to try to get permits for everyone. Maña is embarking from Brussels any day now.

WEDNESDAY, 15 FEBRUARY

I have been in Prague for almost three weeks, with barely a moment to myself. My reason for being here is a training course organized by Wizo. I have now mastered the art of setting a table properly, of serving and clearing, of carrying umpteen plates in one hand, with some set in the hollow of the elbow. I have learned how to deal with inlaid hardwood floors and how to vacuum and wash carpets, and I was introduced to some special cooking techniques and secrets.

But the most important event has been a letter and a notebook containing some of your musical manuscripts, which made me very happy.

The time for my departure seems to be approaching in earnest. Gerti is leaving next Monday. I have done a lot of shopping. Do you really want to hear what I bought? I chose most things with you in mind, except in some instances where practicality and durability were the main consideration. This is the list, up to now: four pairs of shoes (black, navy, brown, plus a brown rubber-soled pair); twelve pairs of stockings, eight underpants, two each of slips and bras and nighties, a brown corduroy raincoat, grey material for a tailored "English" coat, a black dress, fabric for two summer dresses (wine with white polka dots and a blue-white pattern), two blouses (which you may not consider feminine enough), a brown woollen dress – simple and practical; a housecoat – warm and cheap, strictly for myself. I only need to get some small items. All in all, no elegance, just trying to provide for the long haul.

A letter from Berlin arrived yesterday saying that they could perhaps use me and would I fill out the questionnaire. Needless to say, I didn't. Lachnit sent my last monthly cheque and enclosed a note. Erna has been moved to Brünn at her own request. She no longer liked it in Olmütz.

There has also been a clarification about the mysterious contact between you and Erna. I gather that you wrote to her and she merely replied. I am happy and relieved to know this. Perhaps she didn't mention it to me because she assumed you would not wish her to. Or did she merely act in line with her conscience, refusing to be a go-between in a relationship which the Führer would not condone? Hanne, Hanne, stop fretting about her. Forget her.

By contrast, here they – "they" are all women, except for Mr Schwarz, the chef in charge of the cooking course – have been pampering me in all sorts of ways: bringing me sweets, complimenting me on how nice I look in the white maid's cap, and praising the way I am coping with all these manual and menial tasks. Does the "Dr" in front of my name perhaps have something to do with it? Imagine, when Mr Schwarz was going to be away the other day, he asked me, of all people, to take over the course for the day! Then there was the time when the power went off. Everything was topsy-turvy while we were waiting for the inspector. But as it turned out, a knob on the switchboard was loose, and I was able to fix it with a band-aid. When the English lady, chairman of the Lord Mayor's Fund, was here to look us over, I was the only one who could converse with her in English. Before leaving, she asked me for my name. Then there was the time when one of the women had a fall and showed up with a scraped knee, and they called me to attend to her. Suddenly I am being treated like a star, even with regard to cooking! I am flattered and pleased but also puzzled. How come? How shall I fare in England?

The parents and Mimi are my big worry now. No exit in sight. It is as if we were surrounded by prison walls. What will happen to the Jews if there is a war? I cannot bear to think of it. Friedl – our maid in Komotau – writes to us faithfully. The other day she said that our furniture had been auctioned off. But a few days later a message came from the Komotau authorities, in reply to our inquiry I presume, that they had no objection to us moving our things; we could have them picked up by a moving company. Who does one believe?

MONDAY, 20 FEBRUARY, RED-LETTER DAY
THE PERMIT HAS ARRIVED! It was dated 13(!) February 1939, and this is how it reads:

Instructions "R," Paragraph 13(!)

D 2239

Refugee to be admitted to the United Kingdom on condition that she does not enter any employment other than as a resident in service in a private household.

Full name of applicant: Fischl, Hanne

Date of birth: 16.12.1913

Place of birth: Kladno

Single

Nationality: Czechoslovakian

Address abroad: Lobecek 324, Kralupy n.Vlt.

Occupation abroad: Not stated
Signed on behalf of the Co-ordinating Committee for Refugees (Domestic Bureau)

Now my days will be filled with trips to the tailor and shoemaker and shipping agency. Tomorrow I'll have to present myself at the consulate in Prague. But never mind these trivia now! Last Saturday a beautiful letter arrived from America (believe it or not, dated 13 February) saying that the affidavits will soon be on their way.

3

England

1 March – 20 May 1939

This will be the last night in my bed at home. I have packed. The suitcases were bulging so much that I had to buy another. Goodbye old home!

FRIDAY, 3 MARCH

Sitting on deck. The ship is still anchored in Vlissingen Harbour, due to leave in forty-five minutes. It is a radiantly sunny spring day. I have been watching the wild ducks play in the water, dipping in and out. Tall cranes – the inorganic variety – surround us, looking like prehistoric creatures. To me it all seems improbable, a magical landscape. From the train too. This Holland! Everything so dainty, colourful, and cheerful – almost like the interior of a toy shop. The land is entirely flat, crisscrossed by canals that divide it into neat little squares. Here and there a row of poplars marching in a straight line. Then again a windmill, seemingly wound up to turn on and on. And the towns and villages! Clusters of timbered framework houses with peaked gables, each tiny house a different colour, red and blue and green and yellow, with bright shutters and painted balconies. Each more colourful and gay than the next. The buses appear to have come from a toy shop, and the locomotives seem quite jaunty with their shiny brass hats. In each village a church – just like at home; but here they look like miniature cathedrals. And the people also look different somehow: comfortable, rosy, and good-natured. But there is nothing diminutive about them! They are big, up to (and including) their snub noses!

Pages from passport bearing precious permit to land in England, 1939 – with strings attached

I left home yesterday at 5 PM from Masaryk Station. Mutti was crying. Papa looked away. Shall I ever see them again?

The siren is sounding. We are off.

LATER THE SAME DAY, IN LONDON

I am writing this in bed. A moment ago, I stepped out of the bathtub and, exhausted, virtually fell into bed – landing on not one, not two, but three big fat hot-water bottles! (Thank you, guardian angel, whoever you are.) There is much to report but I am too tired to write anything except this greeting to you back home. I hope to wake up early to get caught up.

Good night, Hansel. At last I can call you by name, without fear that my diary may fall into the wrong hands and make trouble.

MONDAY, 6 MARCH, 4:45 PM

Where do I start? Everything was new to me – the Channel crossing, seagulls following us all the way, the arrival in Harwich with hustle and bustle and excitement. But what impressed me most at the point of entry was the attitude of the English customs officers. They actually accepted our word and trusted our honesty (which, it seems to me, bespeaks their own). I was handed a form to read containing a list of articles that were subject to duty. Then the man in uniform asked me if I was bringing in any of them. Yes, I said, I have new shoes and various new garments, but only for my own use. Any presents? No. Camera? Yes. How old? About four years. Good. He didn't even make me open my suitcases. Two young girls – emigrées also – had new typewriters that clearly were subject to duty, but they said they had no money to pay the tax. Normally, the goods would have to be left there until redeemed. Desperate consultations, back and forth. Obviously the customs men wanted to help them, but to allow the typewriters in duty-free would have been contrary to regulations. Finally they came up with a solution: the two women had to give their word of honour not to sell or give away their machines. That was the end of it. (Can you imagine anyone in uniform being that kind – and trusting – and accommodating – and flexible?)

And then there was my porter. Of course I couldn't cope with my luggage by myself. The charge was two shillings, but when I handed him a ten-shilling note (which was all I had), it turned out that he had no change. He mumbled something and was gone. Since the train was about to pull out, I was sure I had seen the last of my money. But at the very last moment, there he was, handing me my eight shillings. If this had been Prague, I would still be waiting for him.

9 PM. I am so behind with this report that I have to cut a long story short. Mrs Warner and her baby twins in Chesterfield were not able to wait for my arrival and have hired someone else. However, not wanting to cancel my engagement and with it my chance to emigrate, they let me come and sent me to Mr Warner's sister instead. Mrs Anderson lives in Sheffield. And here I am, in the Anderson household. Upon arrival, I was told that my job would be that of housemaid, helping with all aspects of the work.

And now to go back and catch up: The train pulled into Chesterfield in pouring rain. A small station, quite a contrast to London's Paddington. A man got out of a chauffeur-driven car and without hesitation headed straight for me. I wonder what made him so certain that I was the person he was waiting for. As his identification, he handed me a letter from home which had arrived for me in the meantime. (I have not mentioned that I spent a night in London, where a friend of cousin Hans Kraus met me and arranged for a room. Even so, the English mail service is phenomenal.)

Mr Warner – yes, it was of course Mr Warner – looked after my luggage and we drove off. In front of a big fish store the car stopped and Mr W got out while I continued on. I thought I had understood that he was sending me to his mother, but I was not sure. His mother? And newborn twins? Soon we stopped again. We crossed the small front garden, the driver opened a door, and I found myself standing in a kitchen. No bell, no knock, no vestibule, not even a double door. A fat woman was doing the dishes. Was this Mrs Warner? "Good afternoon," I said, but she only looked up briefly and continued with her job. Presently the door opened and in walked a pleasant-looking, bespectacled lady – this must surely be Mrs Warner. But no, she led me into another room, where the first person I saw, in an easy chair facing the door, was a one-eyed elderly gentleman. At least I knew this much: he was not Mrs Warner.

And then I saw her. In a bed, which occupied the centre of the room, lay an enormous white-haired woman, unmistakably the mistress of this house. She pointed to a chair by the bedside, inviting me to sit down, and immediately launched into a lecture, of which I understood hardly a word. At first I hoped to slow her down by interjecting a faint "I beg your pardon" from time to time but had to abandon my attempts at following her when I couldn't understand her any better the second time. This much I gathered: she is sending me to her daughter in Sheffield. Today. And I am to come to her (Mrs W) if ever something is not right. After which I was sent to wash hands (my own) and was served tea and some awful meat paste.

I felt like Parsifal, "the dumb knight" on the Mount of the Grail, who was speechless when faced with the sick Kurneval. The entire atmosphere was eerie. It was almost as if there were a veil between me and the world. What a contrast to the hectic times of the last few weeks, during which I was more active and more energetically in charge than I had ever been in my life! When I had been running around, organizing, disposing, preparing, training, doing. And now all I could do was try and guess what was being decided about me and wonder what would happen to me next.

While I was sitting by Mrs Warner's bed, someone turned on the radio, and a rather excited male voice could be heard. Whereupon the one-eyed gentleman jumped up, Mrs W interrupted her speech, they talked excitedly, and he was sent to telephone. "Call up some newspaper for information" – this much I gathered, and my feeling of detachment suddenly left me. To say that I felt nervous would be a gross understatement. After all, all my dear ones were still there. You can imagine my sense of relief when I finally understood what it was all about. Somehow the cricket match in Liverpool had not turned out well. I had arrived in England.

A little later I was sent shopping with Mrs Hall (lady no. 2). It was then I learned that Mrs Warner is paralysed. Around 7 PM they loaded me into a car and shipped me to Sheffield.

CONTINUED ON 7 MARCH

We stopped in front of a big stucco house set in a garden. (All the houses in this area, as I have since found, are big stucco houses set in gardens.) Again no bell, no knocking. This time we didn't step directly into the kitchen, but the kitchen door (onto the corridor) was open, and again the first thing I saw was a fat woman washing dishes. This actually was Mrs Anderson. She greeted me with the same question that up to now everyone else had asked: "How was the journey?" But after my experience in Chesterfield, I knew better than to grope for the right words to describe my trip. Apart from a polite "Very nice, thank you," no real reply was necessary or expected. Mrs Anderson then picked up my little suitcase and insisted, despite my protests, on carrying it while she led me up the staircase to my quarters, an attic room, which I share with the other maid. Within a month they would be moving into a larger place,

she explained, and there my room would not be a garret (not that it matters to me – the more privacy the better!). Talking all the while, she led
me through the rest of the house, or rather, through more of it – the
number of rooms seemed endless – and finally back to the kitchen "for a
cup of coffee."

Writing this two days later, I realize that she made the coffee strictly
for my benefit. It was a grand gesture to please the newcomer and also to
demonstrate her *savoir faire* – of course we know that those stupid continentals prefer coffee! As she proceeded to make it, I watched with increasing fascination. She filled a pot with a mixture of milk and water,
added a heap of ground coffee, and placed the mixture on the gas stove
to boil, after which she stirred it all up and poured it through a sieve.
Along with a generous mug of this, I was offered a rather solid something which she called a "bun." Tired and tense as I was, to work my
way through it all – and anything less would have made me seem rude
and ungrateful – was no mean test of willpower. (Yes, it tasted just as it
sounds.)

To avoid trouble with the other maid, Mrs Anderson explained, I
could not be invited to eat with the family in the dining room but would
eat in the kitchen with Nelly. A Viennese refugee named Paula had
recently been hired as a governess and was to arrive soon.

I took a bath and went to bed. Next day was Sunday. Nelly woke me
at 6:45 and together we dusted downstairs; that is to say, we tidied up
and wiped furniture and floors, the whole vast expanse. I wondered
whether they knew about mops and was told yes, they realized mops and
brooms existed, but wanted us to do it the way it had always been done,
on our hands and knees. Before I forget: first we had a cup of tea, with
milk.

At 8 AM, having finished the "dusting," we had breakfast in the
kitchen, together with Jean, the seven-year-old daughter: tea (with
milk) and toast with butter or "dripping" (beef fat; it tastes awful, and of
course I had the butter.) Then I was to accompany Jean to church.

Anglican church, a children's service. Everyone is handed a songbook.
The organist plays one verse followed by a verse sung by the priest, after

which the congregation joins in. Not unlike a singing lesson in school. After we had sung several hymns, there was a sermon; that is to say, the young priest, one hand in his pocket, walked back and forth in front of the pews and talked. Rather casually. It was actually very nice, and for me, a real experience. Everything simple and seemingly honest and childlike.

Afterwards we went for a walk, and at half past one we had "dinner." Eating with Nelly in the kitchen, I was served an enormous plate filled to the brim. First a sort of pudding followed by mutton with a milky onion sauce, cabbage, and potatoes. Here are the recipes.[1] Place a whole leg of mutton into a pan, put it in the oven, and leave it there for two hours. The cabbage: cover cabbage leaves (whole) with hot water, add salt and baking soda, let it boil for a while, sieve and serve. The sauce: boil onions in water, sieve and add milk. (I managed to eat only very little.) In the afternoon, Nelly, Jean, and I went for a walk.

On Monday morning Mr Anderson came with me to the police station where, according to the conditions spelled out on my entry permit, I was required to present myself. We talked all the way there and back, and I had to strain very hard to understand Mr Anderson. He looks, speaks, and acts exactly the way we continentals imagine Englishmen to look, speak, and behave: tall and slim, and terribly "correct"; and talking as if he had his mouth full of dumpling. He looks quite youthful – especially compared to his fat wife. By profession he is a doctor – or rather, I am told, a "consulting surgeon" (but he is to be addressed as "Mr"). His office hours are two afternoons a week, by appointment only. Otherwise he spends the day in hospitals, doing surgery. This, they say, is on an honorary basis: his income is derived only from consulting. I thought the time when the upper classes were not supposed to work for their living was long past. I can imagine (or can I?) the class of patients he has.

On Monday evening Mrs Anderson announced that from now on I am to be nanny. "What about Paula?" I wouldn't want her to be left stranded in Vienna. But Mrs Anderson assured me, "You are here now. We'll find something else for Paula."

So I have been elevated a notch. Hereafter I am to eat with the family; and by the sound of it, participating in their mealtime ritual is considered to be no trifling privilege. I am no longer "Hanne" but "Nanny." My slippers had to be transferred from the kitchen to the nursery. I must no longer call the manservant "Mr Robertson" but plain "Robertson," and he has to address me as "Miss." If I drink tea in the kitchen, I have to use the "better" dishes. Which reminds me; drinking tea is one of our main occupations: at 8 AM, 9 AM, 11 AM, 3 PM, and 6 PM.

SUNDAY, 12 MARCH

Have been to church again with Jean. I am beginning to understand more of the language. A child reads a segment from the Bible and the priest explains. Today's lesson: You must not sit in judgment over others.

In the afternoon the Andersons were invited out to tea. Jean and I went along for the ride and were supposed to go walking from 4 to 5:30 PM, at which time we were to meet them at a certain place. But when Mrs Anderson finally arrived it was 7 PM, and we were worried, tired, and starving. She couldn't make it any sooner, she said, because the guests included two old ladies and it wouldn't have been proper etiquette to leave before them.

MONDAY, 13 MARCH

The papers tell of increasing tension in Czechoslovakia. The Slovaks want to join Germany. The talk here is of nothing but war, war, war. All morning sirens were howling and bombers flying overhead. Training flights? How I pray for peace!

I got a position for Mimi, or rather, Mrs Anderson did. If only she can get the permit quickly! I am so scared for all my dear ones. Hansl, where are you?

I feel terribly lonesome – surrounded by strangers and imprisoned in a foreign language. They treat me kindly enough. Still, they seem so distant. Worst of all, I don't seem to be able to win over Jean, my seven-year-old charge. I am as patient and kind to her as is humanly possible, but she does anything she can to spite me and delights in getting me into trouble. I couldn't have imagined a child being so malicious and mean. Would you believe that this seven year old has me scared? Is this the experienced teacher who was able to turn those ruffians in Olmütz into loyal friends?

A note from Olga Auerbach, of March 3, forwarded via my parents, in which she gives me the address of a Hungarian businessman, Georg Hilvert, whom I am supposed to remember. He evidently knows me. Did we meet him during our holidays in Abbazia? He now has a business in London and wants to help me get out. I am to send him a curriculum and testimonials. I feel guilty not having let the Auerbachs know that I have left the country, but I have been a little short of time in which to write letters. Still, I should have done so. I wonder what options there would have been through Mr Hilvert.

Another letter, with the funniest bit of news, from the Department of Education in Prague, to inform me that as of 1 January 1939 I have been transferred to the Stephansgymnasium in Prague; and that my term of employment has in the meantime expired and I have been discharged. Salary to run until the end of June. (Do I have to pick it up in person?)

TUESDAY, 14 MARCH

The most awful news. Hitler is marching into Czechoslovakia. Mutti, Papa, Sist, all my dear ones – if only I could help you! I am sick with worry.

THURSDAY, 16 MARCH

A telegram from the parents: "Everybody healthy." Hitler has taken Czechoslovakia. That surely means goodbye to their dream of buying a farm in Canada. The Nazis will hardly release their money. Poor Papa, poor Mutti. What are they to do in their old age?

Here, life goes on as before, and they don't want to see a long sad face, so I try and look cheerful while I work, from 7 AM to 9 PM. This morning I cleaned eight rooms: made beds, dusted, wiped floors, all without a mop or broom, as usual. Then I had to hang out the laundry – again, the hard way. You prop up the clothesline with poles, and for a novice like me, that means a tug of war. Then I prepared tea. Not to forget: first I had to set the table and wait on Jean, who has a bit of a cold. After which I did the ironing. (Mrs Anderson watched as I ironed a pair of her husband's trousers the other day – using a damp cloth, then blowing the steam away, as I remembered our seamstress Kretschmann doing in Komotau. It must have looked rather professional, because ironing has now been added to my duties.) All this before 12:30. What's more, Mrs Anderson was in a black mood and somehow had the idea that I am not working hard enough. But in the afternoon she suddenly noticed my chalk-white face, so she sent me out for a bit of fresh air. My sore toe did not let me enjoy the walk very much.

Yesterday Mr Anderson's secretary was sick, so I typed his letters. Mrs A acknowledged that I had been a great help. Did I say that he is a consulting surgeon with his office at home? I wonder why the English call their surgeons "Mr." Reverse snobbery? On several occasions he has asked my opinion about the political situation, and I get the impression that he rather respects me and likes to talk to me. Today we had almost finished dinner – Jean was still working on hers – when he asked me a question about the situation in Czechoslovakia, whereupon Mrs A got up and abruptly left the room. It was very strange. Mr A stayed a little longer, then left also. It almost seemed as if Mrs A wanted to cut our conversation. Don't tell me she is jealous! That's all I need!

My sadness and sense of desperation really overcame me today. What else is in store for us? I don't see a chance for us to be together, but I cling to the hope, incapable of conceiving of life without you. There seems no way out, no possibility of a good ending. I was so depressed that it made me physically ill. I have to pull myself together. A bundle of misery would be of no use to the Andersons. Good night!

MONDAY, 20 MARCH

Dear diary, I have to come to you for comfort. They treat me like a slave. From 6:45 in the morning until 9 or 10 at night I feel so harried with work that I have barely time to get to the bathroom. What's worse,

Mrs A yells and screams, with the result that I get quite flustered and stupid and understand things the wrong way. It is not easy for me to respond promptly to English commands. It takes a few moments for the meaning to sink in, and when there is such a big rush and commotion as there was today – big laundry and preparation for the move to the other house – I can understand that Mrs A gets impatient. She has a quick temper, suddenly flying into a rage. At first she seemed to me kindness personified, but lately she has been bad tempered and most ungracious. Moreover, Jean cannot stand me, and whenever I enter the room, she attacks me with a stick. When I speak to her, she replies with a torrent of abuse and is forever thinking of ways to hurt and torment me. Above all, she succeeds in getting me in trouble with her mother.

Take yesterday, for instance. All the books were being packed, and at the exact moment when the mountain of books had been piled high on the floor, Jean demanded, "Where is my *Tucks Annual*?"

"I don't know, Jean. I haven't seen it."

Jean, imperiously: "Get me my *Tucks Annual!*"

"How can I, from this mountain? Wait a little, and we'll try to find it."

Jean, yelling: "Are you bringing it or not?"

Realizing that this exchange was getting sillier by the second, I tried to act my age and role: "Not if you talk like that." Whereupon she ran to her mother in the other room.

A few minutes later, Mrs Anderson came in looking cross and ordered curtly, "Nanny, go and wash dishes." As it turned out, the book had been on Jean's bedside table all along, which the little brat knew. And since she had a cold, the fact that I had "refused" to bring it to her was a capital crime. As usual, Mrs Anderson accepted her daughter's version at face value, not giving me a chance to explain.

So Jean continually frames me, always seemingly about trifles, always taking advantage of my insecurity or ignorance, always putting me in the wrong with her mother. Can you imagine a grown woman at the mercy of a manipulative, malicious child? It's probably my fractured English that puts her off, but how can I help that? Actually, being sent to wash dishes was a relief. What in fact I ended up doing was going out in the yard and washing all the pictures in preparation for the move. On a Sunday afternoon! Then I had to pack the books. I finished at 10 PM.

My hands are red and raw, the skin under my nails is cracking, my toe is sore, and my nose suddenly started bleeding – probably from excitement and tension. At the same time, I am annoyed at myself for letting all these trifles get me down when the fear of war hangs over us. Everyone thinks war is inevitable. If only the parents could get out! They at last have a permit for Canada, but now that they are trapped in Hitler's Third Reich, it is unlikely that they will be allowed to export the necessary funds to get them there.

Mimi hopes to come here to Sheffield. I was able to get a position for her through the help of Mr Anderson's secretary, who has taken a very kindly interest in me. She is to work for a Mrs Nichol. No word from Hans or from Hella, our trusty go-between. Everything seems so desolate. No human being in sight. Not being able to talk, I mean really talk instead of trying to communicate in my fractured English. If only I had word from you, everything else could then be borne easily.

TUESDAY, 21 MARCH

Today I am feeling better. Mainly because people were friendlier. All morning I washed dishes: the good china and glass – and there is a lot of it. And in the afternoon I was taken to the new house to unpack the china and wash it again. My hands are chapped, and pus is forming in the cracks.

But Mrs Anderson was civil to me, and I didn't have anything to do with Jean. The one who treats me most fairly is Mr Anderson. He is always the same, always friendly, and I sense that he doesn't want me to feel that I am only a servant. He lets me pass through the door first, opens the car door for me, etc. All little things. But it gives me back some self-respect. Mrs Anderson is very particular about maintaining status. When talking to subordinates, she refers to her daughters, aged seven and nine, as "Miss Jean" and "Miss Margaret" (the latter is away at boarding school), and that's the way the maid has to talk about them and address them. The joke is that Nelly, the maid, and "Miss Jean" fight – I mean physically fight − like alley cats. As Nanny, I may call her Jean, but in talking about her to Nelly, I am to refer to this brat as "Miss Jean." Needless to say, I haven't yet let the words pass my lips! Mrs Anderson never once makes a mistake.

At first I thought the people were good but the food was bad. But I seem to have changed my mind about some of the people, and I've got used to the food. I actually enjoyed today's meal, which was the same as on my first day when I almost choked on it while politely trying to finish. As for the people, I hope I shall get a chance to meet some others. I am beginning to feel claustrophobic and fear that I am losing my sense of humour. My true feelings seem to be showing after all. Mr Anderson asked me today if I was homesick. "No," I lied. I spent the evening with Mrs Anderson and she was very nice. (Did he tip her off?)

FRIDAY, 24 MARCH

A telegram from Mimi: "Have ticket Prague−Bentheim. Send ticket Bentheim−Sheffield." Great! I can hardly wait to have Sist here.

We have moved and there was a lot of work to do. Yesterday I washed windows all day, enormously big ones and so many − it seemed like a hundred of them. It's a huge house. Today I polished furniture, working through from 7 AM to 10 PM. My hand is infected in two places. I had asked whether I might switch my window-washing job with someone else because of my infected hand, but Mrs Anderson suggested I ask someone to dip and wring out the cloth when needed. Can you imagine having to climb down the ladder and find someone to do that? Ridiculous! Of course I did it myself. But what does it matter now that I know that Mimi is on her way out?![2]

SATURDAY, 25 MARCH

I believe that the *Vogelweide Lieder* are being broadcast one of these days. What I wouldn't I give to hear them! I am keeping my fingers crossed.

This has been a good day. Mrs Marchington (Mr Anderson's secretary) had invited me to visit her if and when I could get an afternoon off. So today, after getting up at 6:30, taking tea into their bedroom, and polishing the furniture in all the rooms, I was able to go with Mr Marchington when he called for me at 12:45. They have a pleasant, comfy home. Much, much cosier than the Andersons. Every family here seems to have its own house and garden. We had tea and all sorts of goodies. (Nice change to be waited on as a guest.) There was another guest, a woman, Dr Chem, who spoke a little – very little – German. She invited me to her house. It will be good to get to know some people outside the Anderson household. Even these few hours today have helped me get a little distance from the oppressive Anderson atmosphere, where I feel imprisoned by my ignorance and insecurity – and fear. I shall try not to get rattled when Mrs Anderson turns nasty. My main problem is my limited English. I feel crippled. But what can I do?

She does get mean at times, and she expects an unreasonable amount of work, without allowing me any time to myself during the day. The other day, when a long-awaited letter came from home, I was told to wait till tea break to open it. She obviously is hungry for power – a control freak? And she is cruel. I don't know how long I'll be able to take it.

SUNDAY AFTERNOON, 26 MARCH

I actually got a few minutes off. Mrs Anderson went to lie down and "graciously" gave me permission (Sunday afternoon!) to use the time to organize my things. We are still busy with the aftermath of the move. Most important – I was awakened by a telegram this morning telling me that Sist is arriving tomorrow. Right now she should be floating across the English Channel. It's rather windy out. She tends to be seasick. I hope she took something.

This is how I got the happy news. Having asked her ladyship yesterday what time I would be expected to appear on the scene this morning (this being Sunday) and having been told, "When you feel like it," I was still in bed when she stormed into my room like fury: "Get out of bed! It's almost 8 o'clock!" (It was 7:30.) In her hand was the telegram. It was, of course, unfortunate that she had been disturbed by it, but a fair person would have known that I could not have planned that. I got up, had breakfast, cleaned the consulting room, and since everyone else was still in bed, I found myself temporarily unemployed. So I returned to my room to unpack my own things. But again she barged in.

"Have you unpacked and sorted the tins in the basement yet?"

"Why, no. No one mentioned anything about that."

"My dear child, it will not do that you live in our country and work for yourself instead of your masters. You should have stayed home yesterday afternoon to do your unpacking." I was near tears, but I managed to reply, "I apologize, Madam, but you did suggest yesterday that I should do my unpacking today."

"But not first thing in the morning! Anyway, you could have asked permission." She was obviously looking for a reason to bicker, no matter what I said or did.

Later, when she saw me wipe away tears, she said she was sorry to have treated me badly during the last few days. The move had made her nervous. And "please don't be sad." How can one live with a person who has such violent swings of mood? I don't want to recount all the petty details, but never in my life has a person been as nasty towards me as this woman is. And what makes it worse – even downright humiliating – is that I am trying so desperately to please. Never before have things seemed so hopeless, so joyless, and so bleak. I hear steps outside, which means my break is over.

TUESDAY, 28 MARCH

What I am about to recount will sound like a horror story. Mimi's telegram asking for the railway ticket arrived on Friday. Mrs Anderson kindly telephoned the station on my behalf and was told that the ticket would have to be sent from London. They would see to it immediately and we could expect it to be dispatched by evening. Sunday morning I received this telegram, posted in Prague at 17:33 on Saturday: "Mimi leaving today same train as you arriving Monday Sheffield please come station greetings parents."

I literally jumped with joy, marvelling at the miraculous speed of the postal service: ticket sent Friday, and on Sunday she leaves! I was a little surprised by the unusual wordiness of the telegram: "please," "greetings," "same train as you," instead of the actual time. In high excitement, I met the 2 o'clock train on Monday. My parting word to Mrs Anderson had been, "I am so scared that she may not be on it." Waiting with me on the platform was Mimi's future employer, Mrs Nichol, with her little girl. I was very nervous.

The train arrived – no Mimi. We waited for the next, still no Sist. The next train was due at 4:45, so we drove to the Nichols and later back to the station. Still no Mimi; nor on the next train. I knew she had left. What was I to do? I had to do something. I had brought along the visiting card of the Mr Munk who had met me in London, just in case, so Mrs Nichol took me to the post office to make a person-to-person call. But he had left the office. The person at his home said he had moved three days ago. Back to the station to meet the 8 o'clock train and then again the 9:30 one, the last train from London. Still no Mimi. We went to the police station to report that a refugee had left Prague but had not arrived. They said that she could not have entered Britain because the Sheffield police would have been informed. Great comfort that was! We sent a cable to Uncle Otto (so as not to jolt the parents too much): "Mimi not arrived England. Make inquiries."

This morning, sick with worry anyway, I received two letters from Aunt Ottla[3] with identical content, asking for a letter of invitation for her son Hanuš. Mr Munk, who helped me when I arrived, had been his connection in London, so why was he not inviting his friend? But of course, Munk himself was a refugee; the letter had to come from a British subject. With everyone here up to their ears in their move, I felt utterly helpless, but I knew how desperately urgent this was. I was still pondering what to do, while at the same time wondering what on earth had happened to Mimi, when a letter from cousin Gerti, mailed in London, was handed to me with the text of a telegram she had received on the twenty-seventh, the same day I had received my telegram. It read: "All children at friends in England. Ask lady heartily to wire Friedl invitation. Wants work. Mother." (I wonder what the postal clerks made of Aunt Antschi's quaint English!)

"All children in England!" But what about cousins Margit and Ruth Samel and Hans Pollak? This flurry of telegrams and messages doesn't make sense. Has someone gone berserk, sending these messages? It's a sign of the frantic, desperate situation at home.

I have to close. Mrs Anderson offered me a sleeping pill.

WEDNESDAY, 29 MARCH

Postcard from Mimi's friend Jussl Hoenig, from London, saying that Mimi, Hans, and the Samels are in London. And simultaneously a telegram from home saying that Mimi arrived in London today. Thank God!

THURSDAY, 30 MARCH

Trouble and more trouble with Mrs Anderson. Twice I was on the brink of giving notice or just running away. I work like a dog trying to please her, but she bickers and shouts at me incessantly, and when she flies into one of her rages, which is often, she is most unjust. The child still torments and hits me. Several times when Mrs A witnessed it, she rebuked me instead of Jean, on the assumption that her daughter must have a reason. Sounds improbable, doesn't it? And would you believe it, tonight at 9 PM I had to start vacuuming! Not just some spot, but all the carpets.

Later, same day. Mimi has arrived!!! Once again, I am spending the last night in my bed. I am leaving tomorrow. For the time being, before I find another post, I shall be staying at Dr Nichol's.

FRIDAY, 31 MARCH

How it came about: On Thursday I cried on Mrs Marchington's shoulder about the way they treat me, telling her how Jean kicks and scratches me and beats me with whatever she has at hand, and that she continually manages to get me into trouble with her mother. For instance, Mrs A tells me to have Jean bring her clothes into her mother's room to get dressed there. "And please don't forget the hair ribbon." Jean refuses to take the ribbon, so I carry it into the bedroom myself (Mrs A is not there at this point.) A few minutes later, Mrs A appears, a pained look on her face and sounding exasperated: "You didn't send the hair ribbon after all." When I explain what had happened and suggest that Jean must have hidden it, she becomes very cross – with me! Another time, Mrs A entered the room just as Jean was about to hit me. I was ironing at the time. As usual, she found a reason for my being "punished" by Jean: I had folded the ironing cloth differently from the way they do it. In normal circumstances I would have laughed my head off. But this is not funny. I seem to be caught in my own vulnerability, unable to react normally.

Mr Anderson must have overheard my conversation with the secretary and spoken to his wife about it because some time later a furious Mrs Anderson laid down the law: I am forbidden to talk to Dorothy Marchington or to visit her on my free afternoons.

Friday afternoon brought more trouble over Jean, and this time I decided I had had enough. It was supposedly my free afternoon, but Mrs A sent Jean to town with me to go shopping and then to have tea at a place the child was to take me to. This was supposed to be a treat for me. Why didn't I have the courage to say that I wanted to spend my "free" time by myself? There Jean created a horrible scene. The waitress brought the tea but forgot to bring Jean's milk. To be honest, I didn't always understand what the child was saying, and I may have missed her order for milk, so this part was of course my fault, as usual. Anyway, it prompted her to fly into a rage, attacking me with knife and fork, yelling, "Give me my milk!" and scratching my face. The people around us jumped up, stunned at this spectacle. Jean seemed completely out of control while I, mortified, tried to subdue her. Imagine a nanny fighting with her charge in a proper English tea room!

Back home, as soon as we stepped in the door, I reported what had happened and showed Mrs A my scratched face. She sent Jean to bed and then lit into me, shouting that it was a mistake to enter the room complaining. What a way to be greeted!

But I was in no mood to discuss etiquette. "Sorry," I said, "but it had to be told in front of the child or you would not have believed me."

Her reply: "This must never happen again."

"Quite, Madam, I don't believe this can go on."

"I beg your pardon?" She was genuinely taken aback, suddenly realizing that I meant it. "Go now and meet your sister."

Without another word, I left. From the station, I accompanied Mimi to the Nichols. Dear Mimi. And good kind Nichols, so calm and reasonable and normal. While I was there, Mrs A telephoned and it was agreed that I would look for another job.

FRIDAY, 14 APRIL

I am lying in a comfortable double bed in a beautiful hotel, and the sea is roaring under my window. From 10 AM until about 4 PM we drove through lovely countryside. Last night I dreamed that I was in a theatre somewhere, sitting in the balcony, and the hall below was filled with people from Komotau. And suddenly I spotted your blond topknot among them and waited for you to wink at me surreptitiously. But you waved quite openly, with a big smile, and I ran to you and hand in hand we walked through the crowded room. When I woke up I was sadder than ever. I wonder why I don't hear from you. Hella wrote that she forwarded my letter and pictures. In your last letter – it seems such a long time ago – you said, "See you in summer."

But I almost forgot. I have yet to report what happened in the meantime. On Saturday, when I went back to the Andersons to pack my suitcase, Mrs Anderson insisted that I work till noon. That, she said, was the custom. Okay, why not? We began to talk and she became her friendliest self, turning on all her charm. When she asked me to try it for another week, I couldn't very well refuse. (You know me – when people are nice to me, I turn to jelly.) But the Nichols, to whom I returned later that day, urged me to look for another place.

That very afternoon I was interviewed by a Mrs Cunnington, who needed someone to take care of her two boys. She hired me on the spot. Back at the Andersons for the intervening days as I had promised, I was asked to reconsider. Would I not be willing to go to their summer place in Anglesey with the children? (Their four older children are away at school.) But I was adamant. On Wednesday I moved.[4]

That was nine days ago, and now we are holidaying for a few days in Blackpool. The Cunningtons treat me in a civilized manner. I feel like an adult human. It's wonderful. The boys are very nice, Michael almost six, Nigel three and a half.

I am too tired to go on. Good night.

SUNDAY, 16 APRIL

All night I heard the waves roar. The sea is awesome: unfathomable, beautiful.

THURSDAY, 20 APRIL, BACK IN SHEFFIELD

Mail has arrived for me at the Andersons. I am to pick it up tomorrow. (Why not today? Mrs Anderson doesn't relinquish power easily.) I can hardly wait. There has been no word from Hans or Hella for over five weeks – no reply to my last three letters.

FRIDAY, 21 APRIL

A letter from Hans! Also one from Hella. The broadcast was on the eighteenth. I am so happy. Everything suddenly looks different. Hans wants to come here in the summer. I mustn't let myself think of it.

SATURDAY, 22 APRIL

Spent time with Mimi. Good news from home – they are getting a permit for Canada. And bad news – the Germans aren't issuing any exit or transit visas.

Mimi had a letter from the Cunard White Star Limited, Canadian Settlement Department, dated 20 April. We are to appear as soon as possible in London for an interview and medical examination. The final paragraph: "Please ensure that you carry with you any passport or identification papers you have in your possession. It is important you come to London early next week, as until you are examined we cannot have the Canadian Government go ahead with the arrangements for your parents."

FRIDAY, 28 APRIL

We were in London two days ago. What will happen now? Do I have to leave for Canada before I have the chance to meet Hans here? I asked the Canadian representative whether it was essential that we all travel together (did not dare mention "later"), and he said that the government "doesn't like it." Doesn't like what? I didn't dare probe further for fear of hurting the parents' case by saying the wrong thing. Yesterday I wrote to Hans (via Hella) for advice in case I have a choice with regard to my date of departure.

A farm in Canada! That might be the solution for the two of us! Couldn't you come for a visit, for good? Do you remember how we day-dreamed of a farm?

During the interview in London, Mimi and I both presented ourselves as willing, sturdy farmhands. Could we milk? Yes, we said. (I assume it can be learned quickly enough.) Did we ever work in a factory? Mimi had recently been trained for a few weeks in Uncle Louis' glove factory in Bärringen in preparation for Canada, but lest a positive answer might mark us as possible "bolshies," she didn't mention it.

MONDAY, I MAY

Letter from Mutti. They are already packing and are now "only" waiting for passports and exit visas. Mimi and I somehow have to find the money for our ocean passage. Perhaps the Refugee Committee might help. Hans Pollak will have to inquire.

THURSDAY, 4 MAY

Out of the blue, Mr Auerbach just called me from London. He only wanted to say hallo – they are all in Paris – but he added that if I ever needed money or anything else, I must let him know. The passage! I seem to have a guardian angel after all.

MONDAY, 8 MAY

A letter from Uncle Charles, sent from Paris on 6 May. He had just had an excited message from Maña that Mimi and I had done something

Hanna's parents Ella and Adolf Fischl, on Adolf's fiftieth birthday, Komotau 1935

terribly stupid: "As you know, Louis received the permits on condition that the men would work on farms while the women would make gloves in his factory. We understand that both of you have declared to the Cunard people that you cannot sew gloves." It goes without saying that we didn't know these conditions. Nor were we asked the question, at least not directly.

"This was immediately relayed to Canada, and all permits are to be cancelled. Do you know what that means? It means that your parents as well as the Pollaks and Samels will be trapped where they are. People arriving here, and non-Jews who dare to write, are reporting ghastly things. Jews are arrested daily. In Pilsen[5] hundreds were taken away while we were still there, and last week 153 more Jews were arrested in the city alone. Before our departure, I saw several such 'work parties' marching past under heavy police guard. Even if you don't want to go to Canada, why spoil it for the others? Louis is exasperated, and it is questionable whether he will be able to do anything about it. He could not get in touch with you directly because he does not have your address" ... etc, etc. There followed another page of recriminations – as if we needed to be told how awful this was – ending with, "Canada was the last chance. There is no other way out now. Even Ecuador has closed its doors." Do I have to say that I was desperate?

Of course I told Mrs Cunnington, and she promptly took matters in hand. "What nonsense! This is a misunderstanding. You must simply explain to the Cunard people," and she sat down and did just that. In her elegant, beautiful English, she composed a letter, in my name, telling it exactly as I had reported it to her. I signed "my letter" and sent it off. Then I wrote to Hans – now John – Pollak (near London), to Mimi who is with the Nichols in Scotland for two weeks, to Uncle Charles in Paris, and to Uncle Louis (Hotel Windsor, Montreal).

WEDNESDAY, 10 MAY

Two letters from home. Poor Mutti, poor Papa.

THURSDAY, 11 MAY

Letter from Cunard. Thank God, the matter has been cleared up, the permits restored. "My" letter did the trick. Dear, dear Hilda Cunnington! How can I ever thank you enough![6]

WEDNESDAY, 17 MAY

The morning mail brought a letter from Hans. I am happy and sad at the same time. At noon, a dear letter from Mutti. And in the evening, a phone call from Mr Auerbach. He is lending me the money for the passage to Canada.

Now I am sitting in front of the fire, rereading your letter. Yes, I have seen the sea and York Cathedral. But all seems empty and lonesome without the one who can make wood talk and paper sing. And now I am to move even farther away, beyond the big water.

Dorothy Marchington wrote me a very nice note from Hatch End, somewhere on the south coast of England, where she is holidaying. She lost her job with the Andersons over her involvement with me but assures me that she is feeling much better now and had meant to make a break anyway. She hopes that I am happy with the Cunningtons. I certainly am!

Ashdell Grove, Sheffield, home of the Cunnington family

Life at Ashdell Grove, the Cunnington home, is an enriching, fascinating experience. This is a large house[7] which they are running as a home for paying guests. We would probably call it a *Pension*. Interesting people among them. In the evening, after the boys are in bed, I have a standing invitation to join the adult party downstairs. Mrs Cunnington's parents, Mr and Mrs Noble, also live here. Both very tall and slim and civilized, they treat me with consideration and kindness (true to their name!). They help in running the house and also spell me off with the boys when necessary.

Mr Cunnington (Bill) is a math teacher in a grammar school and has to travel by car to a school some distance away in a neighbouring town. I don't remember ever having met such an obviously happy, devoted couple. Hilda Cunnington is in charge of a family-planning clinic. Says she wants to share her happiness with others. It seems a rather progressive, courageous undertaking. Birth control is a delicate subject here too, almost as taboo as on the continent. But in England the movement is being pioneered by a certain aristocratic lady, which makes the cause more acceptable. I was taken along to one of their (evening) meetings. Husband Bill came as well. He often joins Hilda, mainly lecturing, I believe, and counselling.

The boys are sweet, especially Michael. Nigel is a little rascal, though he looks like an angel, with the blond curl on his forehead. A strict routine is being maintained with regard to the boys. Mrs Cunnington has very definite ideas about what's good for them. They have to go to bed at 6 PM, right after their tea and bath; and since that means that they are awake early (any time from 5 AM on), before the adults want to be disturbed, a toy or book is placed by their bedside – something different every day – along with a glass of orange juice, and they are expected to amuse themselves until it's time to get up. And they actually do. My room is near theirs, in the nursery wing, separated by a thin wall.

Mrs Cunnington believes that "the early evening sleep is the best," hence this peculiar regime. But it is also nice for us adults as it gives us the evening free. The rest of the household have a late supper and sit around the fire. All of which includes me. What a change from the nightmare existence at the Andersons! In retrospect, I can hardly believe that this grown-up woman, who had been able to control classrooms full of students, sometimes in very trying situations, had been defeated by a seven-year-old child.

Today was my free afternoon. Dr Row and Dr Thomas, two of the Cunnington guests, took me on a tour of Sheffield University, especially the chemistry laboratories where they work. A different world, certainly lacking the picturesqueness and patina of my Prague alma mater, but how kind of my two guides to do this! Do they want to let me feel that I have not left the realm of academia for good?

SATURDAY, 20 MAY

Letter from home. Mimi is to leave at once because Uncle Louis needs her. Dear Hans. I shudder to think that I am about to place an ocean between us, yet it seems the only way for you and me to be together. But do you really want to come? Can you actually bring yourself to abandon

Hilda Cunnington, 1939 (courtesy Nigel Cunnington)

your spiritual home and your public – and, most important of all, the German language? And just for me? I had to leave, but you don't. Your letter said that I am fortunate in having to worry only about my life. I know what you mean, although you don't elaborate. For you, as I have known all along, music comes first. Or rather, your commitment to creating music. It is almost as if you bore your creative gift as an assignment to be carried out, a burden to be endured. But then, in the end, you will have created something lasting, while I shall merely have grown old.

I just spent a most pleasant evening with a young Russian woman, Kupara Barkett. It was all rather unexpected. Michael had invited a friend, little Ian Barkett, to play with him this morning. I organized some games for the boys, kept Nigel out of their hair, and told them fairy tales – my recently revised, rather tame version of the tales. For I have recently found that with eager ears hanging on my every word while I carefully pick my way through English equivalents for the familiar idiom – so familiar that one hardly thought of the actual meaning – the good old Grimm's *Hausmärchen* suddenly seem to lose their innocence. I cannot bring myself to tell Michael and Nigel that Hansel and Gretel were sent into the woods by their parents in the hope that they would never return. Or that in the end they shoved the wicked witch – never mind how wicked – into the oven. Or that stepmothers are bad. And how does one say "Knusper-knusper – Knäuschen, was knuspert an meinem Häuschen? Der Wind – der Wind – das himmlische Kind"? So

I find myself continually modifying the tales. But despite these domesticated – and, I am sure, less interesting – variants, the boys keep asking for more.

But to return to today's events. Not long after little Ian left, Mrs Cunnington had a call from his father, who is a lecturer in Russian at the university. Ian had told him that the Cunningtons had a new German-speaking nanny. Was she by any chance an emigrée? Still later, just after I had put the boys to bed, Mrs Barkett appeared to invite me to their place for the evening. Kupara is a teacher, about my age. Of Russian parentage, she studied and taught in

Hanna, photographed by Hans Feiertag, 1937

Germany for two years; her German is perfect. At present, she is working on a book about Russian folk music. A very nice, warm, stimulating couple – the lively conversation made the evening just fly by. It gave me a real boost.

4

Canada

3 June 1939 – December 1941

SATURDAY, 3 JUNE [1939]
My last night in Europe. Tomorrow we set sail. In the end, everything went very quickly. The Cunningtons have been simply wonderful. Hilda and Bill had planned a holiday but cancelled it to help me. They have done more for me than I can say. They are going to drive Mimi and me to Southampton. Hilda and I have grown very close. Last night, she sat by my bedside and we talked through half the night. There was so much to catch up on. Just now Mr Cunnington phoned to thank me for being so good to the children and making them so happy.

SUNDAY, 4 JUNE
When we came aboard ship, a gift-wrapped package of Yardley soap was handed to me, together with a telegram from the Cunningtons saying, "Loving wishes for the future." We are at sea now, moving away from everything that ever mattered. As the flag was hoisted, I said goodbye once more to all our favourite places, one by one. And now there is water all around me and seagulls above me. Marvellous.

Why it went so quickly: There was considerable back and forth about the tickets – not worth reporting. Suffice it to say that only two days ago did we learn that we were to leave today. Meanwhile, there had been another worrisome hurdle. Sist was recalled to London for another medical checkup. They had found something in her eyes that would make her ineligible as a Canadian immigrant. In the end, they allowed her to pass to be re-examined in Canada. (What on earth can be wrong? We never knew of any problem.)

The ship is large and beautiful, called, of all things, *Alaunia*![1] Mimi and I share a cabin, of course. There is a group of Sudeten German Social Democrats on board, a Jewish family, and the rest of the passengers are English. I have talked to many of them. Everyone smiles at us.

A comforting thought: it evidently isn't all that difficult to cross the ocean. Hilda has invited Hans and me to their house if we want to meet in England.

MONDAY, 5 JUNE. DAY 2 ON THE *ALAUNIA*

Many of the passengers were already seasick early this morning. My turn came a little later, but I "fed the fishes" only once. The seagulls have deserted us and we are now on the high seas. I saw golden waves reflecting the noonday sun. I saw a blood-red sunset. Still later, I saw an enormous ball of fire rise, then shrink, turn yellow, and become old friend moon. I stood by the railing and saw frothing waves and fish jumping.

TUESDAY, 6 JUNE. DAY 3 ON THE *ALAUNIA*

I woke at 4 AM and peered through the porthole. My seniority gives me the privilege of the lower bunk which, Mimi warns me, may turn out to be a mixed blessing next time she gets one of her sudden seasick spells. It was a fabulous sight, and I mean that literally. Like a fairy tale: blue-green waves topped with white points as far as the eye could see, and above them a luminous pink dawn. Sea, sea, sea. A miraculous, breathtaking experience.

We are a happy group of passengers, a very mixed bunch. No one knows anything about anyone else. All that matters is whether a person is pleasant, friendly, and a good sailor. Mimi and I find ourselves part of everything that is going on, and if we happen to be absent, someone comes to fetch us. In the evening there is dancing. Two German passengers are providing the music with a fiddle and an accordion.

The meals are great, starting with seventeen choices of breakfast food. I like something they call "cornflakes" so much that I haven't brought myself to try any of the others. They are crisp, crunchy flakes, eaten with sugar and cream – yummy! I must remember the new word: "cereals." I think it has something to do with the Roman goddess Ceres. The other meals also contain so many tempting offerings that it's difficult to make a choice. And the ice cream! The young Greek waiter has taken a fancy to us two "lone" young women and brings us second and even third helpings of ice cream.

A bloody sunset, supposed to mean storm.

WEDNESDAY, 7 JUNE. DAY 4

I was woken again and again by the foghorn. An eerie sound. Now, in daylight, sea and sky seem as one and the siren continues to wail at regular intervals. We stay inside in the lounges.

I won ten shillings (seventy crowns)! Yesterday, in one of the contests organized by the ship's crew, we were asked to put in sixpence each and guess how many knots the boat had travelled in the past twenty-four hours. Since I didn't have a clue and didn't have sixpence to spare, I was not going to participate when an Englishman put in the money in my name and suggested, "Write down 182." At dinner the steward announced that the correct figure was 182. My first win ever. A good omen?

THURSDAY EVENING, 8 JUNE

We are standing still. It feels weird. Apparently we are close to icebergs. The daily newssheet tells about the king and queen touring Canada and the enthusiastic reception they are receiving everywhere. It gives me a strange feeling that this is to be my country.

SUNDAY, 11 JUNE

At last we are on the move again! For almost three days we were surrounded by fog as if by a solid wall. A while ago, when I stepped out on deck, I was almost blinded by the brilliance. The sea is blue again, and, for the first time, towering waves are rolling along, spraying foam all the way up into my face. The sea, it seems, has suddenly come to life. It feels great! Many of the passengers are seasick. Except for the second day, when Mimi and I felt queasy, we haven't missed a meal. We play games, walk on deck, sit around. The less one does, the lazier one gets. It's time we landed!

I spend much of the time watching the others. Besides English and Canadian travellers and the Social Democrats from the Sudeten, there is a group of peasants from the Ukraine. We are usually with the English speakers. And without trying to take centre stage, we keep finding ourselves holding court. One Harry, one Kenneth, and a George are trying to flirt with me. I suppose this "goes with the territory" during an ocean passage. Needless to say, they don't get much encouragement from me. But it does seem as if the worries of the past and the concerns for the future are somehow suspended for the time being.

WEDNESDAY, 14 JUNE

We see land! Canada! Brilliant sunshine.

Later. All day we sailed up the St Lawrence. The loveliest, most vivid green on both banks of the wide river. Never before have I seen grass of such a vibrant green. Is it simply the contrast between the grey days behind us and the lush green of early June – or symbolic of greener pastures ahead? Our destination is Montreal, but first we stop in Quebec to take immigration officers on board.

This morning we had to line up for yet another medical examination and passport control. At first I thought of it as routine, but when I noticed the doctor examining people's eyes, I got nervous, remembering the reservations they had about Mimi in London. Someone ahead of us was apparently having a problem. Worrisome. By the time our turn came, I was inwardly trembling. While we stepped up together, I finished my sentence to Mimi, desperately trying to sound casual and nonchalant. The doctor was still looking at the paper before him. Our records? I was continuing my quiet chat with Sist when he looked up and broke in, "Where did you learn English?"

"In Sheffield."

"How many years were you there?"

"Three months."

"I suppose you speak French too?"

"Yes, some." Whereupon he talked to me in French for a minute or so. And that was it – I think he forgot that he had not examined us.

Next came passport control. The officer looked at our papers and broke
into a smile. He knows Uncle Louis well: "Please give him my regards."
Then a woman stuck a blue ribbon on our lapel to indicate that we were
"lone sheep."

And that was it. And now I must go and watch the glorious sunset.
Au revoir in Prescott!

THURSDAY, 15 JUNE, PRESCOTT

So here I am at the other side of the world. Prescott is a small town in
the province of Ontario. Across the river – yes, it is the mighty
St Lawrence – lies the Unites States. Knowing that the skyline we see
on the other bank belongs to Ogdensburg, New York, gives one a funny
feeling.

The Fischls live in a big, beautiful house, which is empty as yet except
for pictures and Persian carpets and a few borrowed chairs. They seem to
have been befriended by a lively circle of local dignitaries. Last night
Mayor Horan's family (wife and two grown daughters) and Father
Briceland, the vivacious young Catholic priest, came to welcome Mimi
and me. They acted as if they were old friends of the Fischl family.

How Lea² has grown! But she still likes to ask more questions than
one can (or wants to) answer. Maña is sick today. During the night she
was in great pain with a gallstone attack. The doctor called this morning
and gave her an injection. Now she is asleep. We have arrived at the
right moment! She has lost a lot of weight since I last saw her in Kralupy
– almost twenty kilos, she says. She looks as slim as she was as a young
bride.

Besides learning to make gloves, I am to help out in general where I
can. This means, for the time being, looking after the household.

SUNDAY, 18 JUNE

This is the day of your broadcast. I wonder what is being performed –
perhaps even my radio play on Walther von der Vogelweide. You said in
your letter that I would be pleased. We have no radio, and even if we had

been able to find a short-wave radio in Prescott – and we scurried around looking for one – I would not have known when to listen. I assume that you couldn't give me the information in case the letter was opened by the censors, but I did keep my fingers crossed, figuratively speaking.

We went to church today, the United Church of Canada. In order to qualify as Canadian immigrants, we had to declare ourselves nondenominational. I had no problem with that. I never did feel particularly Jewish. It was only other people who saw us as different. And since people here seem to assume that one attends a church ("Which church do you go to?" is a common question), Uncle Louis wants us to join this Canadian one. I am told that it's called the United Church of Canada because it was formed through a merger of Methodists and Presbyterians and because it is a strictly Canadian institution. This smorgasbord of creeds and the concern with religious affiliation is something new to us. I don't recall the church playing such a part in people's daily lives in the Old Country. At least, not where we lived. Anti-Semitism there is not based on religion. Will it be different here? Obviously, Canada is not free of it either. Will membership in the United Church allow us to begin our new lives without a strike against us? And with success or failure depending only on our own efforts and attitude – and luck?

MONDAY, 19 JUNE

Maña is still sick. Mimi is to start in the factory tomorrow and I am to continue to keep house here.

Last night Mimi and I called on the Fischers, Anton and Rudolf Fischer, the glove-maker brothers with their families who worked for Louis in Bärringen and whom he brought with him. As Social Democrats they had to run from the Nazis too. Through them I met a high school teacher, Mr Shevers, and his wife – a pleasant young couple. He said he had been looking forward to meeting me, and he proved that this was not mere talk by presenting me with a calendar of the University of Toronto. I should have a good chance of getting a position there as a teacher of German, he thought.

SUNDAY, 25 JUNE

Attended church again this morning. I rather enjoy hearing Mr Coburn preach – a new experience for me. He called a few days ago, in his ministerial capacity, to invite Mimi and me. And yesterday his daughter Margaret, about our age, came with her car to pick us up for a drive. But the van with the furniture – the Fischls' possessions from home – had in the meantime arrived and we were busy unpacking and moving furniture. So this afternoon we in turn called on Margaret to see if she wanted to join us for a walk, but we got so involved in conversation with the Coburn family that the afternoon flew by. I really like Mr Coburn. He seems wise, gentle, kind, and very interested in us. He promised to correct my English, especially my pronunciation. After church, several people spoke to us, invariably starting with "How do you like Canada?" and ending with "Please come to see us."

Two days ago the Davidsons drove up and packed Mimi and me into their car to show us the countryside. Mr Davidson is the local banker. They have a daughter just a little younger than us.

TUESDAY, 4 JULY

A whole week has gone by since my last entry and we are settling into a routine. I am still needed in the house. This is the pattern: Up at 7:15 AM, I get breakfast (coffee, cocoa, cornflakes, orange juice, toasted bread – quite different from our European breakfast of coffee and fresh-baked rolls) and tidy up downstairs, which means the entrance hall, living room, and dining room. Maña arrives on the scene at nine, after which I wash the dishes and clean the four bedrooms and bathroom. Then comes shopping and cooking. Today there was also laundry. If there is no ironing, I am out of the kitchen by 4 PM. Supper at 6 PM, dishes again, and at 8:30 the great round-up begins when the children have their baths and are put to bed. Up to now, we have had visitors on most evenings: the Horans, Father Briceland, Margaret Coburn. (What did they do for excitement before we came?) But it does feel good! Still, I soon shall have to consider planning my own life a little.

Mutti and Papa are still waiting for the Gestapo to issue their exit visas. Meanwhile, the political situation is getting more worrisome by the minute. Any day now Hitler may occupy Danzig. That would mean war. I shudder.

People keep asking whether Mimi and I are twins. (Is that the polite way of finding out who is the elder?) It's flattering. If only I could make time stand still!

I find Mr Coburn's sermons helpful. It is a relief to get some distance from the small things which seem to engulf one. Maña, whom I have always admired because she was such a generous, magnanimous person who tended to "think big," now appears to be fretting about trifles. At least that's what they seem to Sist and me. We find ourselves watching what mood she is in, and her frame of mind in turn affects Louis. I had never realized what a strong influence she exerts. Of course, I know that she and Louis must be under enormous pressure, trying to establish the business in very different and difficult circumstances, and then there's her physical pain as well as the worry about her parents and brother, who are still waiting to leave Czechoslovakia. Luckily, Mimi and I have each other to lighten the atmosphere when it gets tense. We do have a lot of laughs. Above all, we never forget how indebted we are to them.

WEDNESDAY, 5 JULY

The heat is oppressive. Everyone is bathed in perspiration. In the middle of the afternoon, while I was still ironing, Margaret Coburn dropped in and persuaded me to join her for a swim. It didn't take much persuasion. We drove about three miles downriver and had a good long swim. I was back in time to finish the ironing and make supper.

I am happy to report that my efforts at cooking are appreciated! Today Maña again praised my tasty meals. She has gained three kilos since we came.

Last night we were invited to a party organized by the Catholic church. Father Briceland passed us around. At one point I heard someone comment behind my back, "Lovely girls." Now Miss Mitschkerle and I call each other "lovely girl."

THURSDAY, 6 JULY

No relief from the heat. Mimi and Maña seem to be suffering more than I. After supper, Margaret drove us and the children [Maña and Louis' children, Lea and Johnnie] a long way up the river. Beautiful sunset.

It is now almost midnight and too hot to sleep. I am reading the Michelangelo biography by Romain Rolland.

FRIDAY, 7 JULY

Happy day! A letter from Hans, forwarded from England. You are glad that I am safely away. But how about you?

WEDNESDAY, 12 JULY

A lot has happened. On Saturday, Mimi and I, Lea and Johnnie were taken to a Sunday school picnic in Brockville. Organized by "our" church. A picnic to Canadians is important business. You drive your car into the countryside for the purpose of eating outdoors. For this you need to bring sandwiches, salads, bowls full of vegetables, fruit, cakes, cookies, various hot and cold drinks, and you also need plates, cutlery, and a tablecloth. No, dear Hansi, I am not exaggerating. You set out at 3 PM and you return at 7 PM.

On Sunday – the next day – we had a picnic of sorts with the competition; together with Father Briceland, we were all invited to the Horans' summer cottage. Father Briceland seems to be a fixture in the Horan household. Lots of noise and merriment. Of course, we swam in the St Lawrence.

On Monday, Uncle Charles, Aunt Lise, Lilly and Felix[3] arrived directly from Paris. They stayed with us for two days. In addition, four men came to dinner last night, so we were fifteen around the table. And I was the cook. I am completing my apprenticeship in a hurry! Actually, everything worked well. It's good to be useful. But I wouldn't want to do this forever. The Munks have now moved into a hotel; or rather, into *the* hotel.

THURSDAY, 13 JULY

Once again, the thirteenth is our lucky day. Uncle Louis returned from Ottawa, where he had an interview with the Almighty: Mr Blair of the Immigration Department. The great news is that Louis can get entry permits for others interested in joining our little colony here. I asked him whether he has anyone in particular in mind, and he looked at me for a few seconds before answering, very slowly, "Isn't there someone you have in mind?" Dear Uncle Louis. How can I get in touch with you quickly, without getting you into trouble? I am writing immediately, via my parents and also via Mali Weisbach and Hella.

The Canadian entry permits state that the parents, the Pollaks, and the Steiners[4] will be goat breeders. To supply the glove factory!

SUNDAY, 23 JULY

Letter from John Pollak (using his anglicized name), saying that our people are expecting their exit visas soon; and that each family will be receiving a thousand dollars from the Czechoslovak Committee in London towards buying a farm, in addition to having their passage paid.

A lot of company. Pleasant, though at times not leaving me time to myself. We are often with the Coburns and I find that stimulating. Yesterday Mr Coburn read me some poems. Afterwards he asked me to try to interest his daughter in English literature. I played their piano a little – just so-so, I felt. It's a long time since I last practised. The other day, Mr Coburn tested me with a word list from *Reader's Digest*. You had to indicate which of the several meanings was correct. They were mostly what he called big – not very common – words, which made it all the easier because most of these "big" words have recognizable Latin or Greek roots. Mr Coburn was visibly impressed. I had done better than his daughter. So I explained (after all, I hadn't meant to bluff, nor did I want to compete with Margaret) how I had merely guessed the meanings from their Latin and Greek origins. But my explanation had the opposite effect from what I intended. He was even more impressed.

MONDAY, 24 JULY

They say that this is the hottest day of the year. Margaret Coburn showed me an anthology of English poems, a textbook used in the schools, and was surprised that I already knew several of them almost verbatim. I had chosen them for you as possible song texts. I am delighted that I seem to have made the right choices – but also somewhat embarrassed about the inflated opinion the Coburns are getting of me.

TUESDAY, 25 JULY

Mimi and I were invited to supper at the Coburns. Afterwards they made me read some poems out loud, and later Mr Coburn read some of his own – rich in kind thoughts and verities and wisdom, nicely rhymed, and well meant. Great poetry it is not.

WEDNESDAY, 26 JULY

Cable from Prague: "Odjíždíme dnes, v sobotu Southampton [Leaving today, Southampton Saturday], Ada, Pollak, Samel." Mimi brought the cable into the kitchen and we both broke down and cried.

THURSDAY, 27 JULY

The Fischls now have a real housekeeper, so I spent my first day in the factory. It went quite well. Mrs Frappier, the supervisor, has big plans for me. She wants to train me to take her place. This is not as flattering as it may sound. They know that I will not be staying forever, and it may be easier to train a supervisor than a worker.

The first goats have arrived! The local paper made a big fuss with reports of this "shipment of goats." There are actually four of them, father, mother, and two babies; they were brought here all the way from the next concession, about four miles from Prescott. Half the population of Prescott has meanwhile shown up, by car and on foot, to view the goats. We keep a straight face and hope the goatherds to go with them will arrive next week as scheduled.

I am concerned about Mimi. She doesn't look well. The heat and the tense atmosphere in the factory may be getting to her. She seems harassed and nervous. I miss her sense of humour.

MONDAY, 31 JULY

Louis scolded me for not having mentioned sooner that Mr Auerbach might consider coming to Canada. People with money can be brought out easily, he said. I wrote to Mr Auerbach at once.

TUESDAY, 1 AUGUST

More new friends: Isabel Elliott, the daughter of our landlord, a high school teacher. She called me to invite us for a drive. Mimi, Lea, Johnnie, and I have just returned from a beautiful outing. We saw a gorgeous sunset and later watched the moon rise above the water. Fabulous.

SUNDAY, 20 AUGUST

These have been two eventful and busy weeks. The parents, Aunt Milly, and Margit have come and all the Pollaks — Aunt Antschi and Uncle Otto, John, Fred (no longer Friedl), and Gerti.[5] Papa and Mutti are looking quite well and are overjoyed because we are together again. Everybody is here except Ruth, who chose to stay in England. They also came on the *Alaunia* and were surprised that some of the crew remembered the two Fischl sisters.

The very next day a reporter arrived. Great to-do about me. The story that appeared in the local paper was headlined "PhD Happy Making Gloves." It was followed by another a day or two later. Needless to say, "happy making gloves" is a bit of an overstatement. I don't exactly rejoice at sitting behind a sewing machine from 8 AM to 6 PM, with one hour off at noon, literally glued to the chair with perspiration, while fending off mosquitoes and flies, and trying to cope with a machine that won't cooperate, as well as with leather that sticks to the fingers and, above all, my two left thumbs.

Maña and Louis Fischl on a visit to Prague, 1964 (courtesy John
Fischl)

Working with leather is stressful at best, even for the experienced, because mistakes are rarely correctible; every stitch leaves a hole. Louis and
Maña are understandably nervous, trying to establish (or maintain) their
reputation as first-rate producers of fancy kid gloves. They have to pay
high wages (minimum wage $17 a week), yet hardly anything is being
produced that meets the required standard. Most of us are mere appren-
tices. It's no wonder the atmosphere is tense, here and there erupting in
an explosion. And when that happens, everyone cowers. Mimi is particularly vulnerable. After working fast and well at the beginning, she
seems to have trouble now, and Maña gets exasperated and is very hard
on her. Poor Sist. I am better off because they didn't expect much of me
to begin with, treating me as the "intellectual." The reporter promised to
find out from the university whether my qualifications as a teacher
would be valid here.

MONDAY, 21 AUGUST

Hans Feiertag is twenty-eight today. I celebrated by bicycling a long way out by the river. There was a breathtaking sunset. I had a letter ready, which Lilly had offered to have mailed in Paris, but it seemed too dangerous. Supposing it was opened! Similar messages have arrived from Hella, mailed in Bärn, and from Bertl Steiner in Prague, who forwarded the letter you sent to the parents. I wish you were here, though I worry about what you would do if you were. Culturally, this seems a wasteland. We were at a piano concert the other night, and it was awful. I have not had any reply to my last three letters. Did they reach you? It is almost a year since we were last together, walking through the night from Nové Stašecí to Krupá. I still see the hop gardens emerging out of the morning mist. And the dismal station waiting room. And the bend in the road above the station. After that, except for a glimpse from a distance, I saw you only once. You were talking to someone in front of the house of Professor Killiches in the Plattnerstrasse, wearing your beige pullover. I don't even know if you saw me cycling by on the other side of the road, almost falling off the bike as I was trying to take a good look. I didn't know that that would be the last one. Happy birthday!

SUNDAY, 27 AUGUST

The first night on our farm.[6] A nice red-brick house. Our own land as far as I can see. Too tired to continue tonight.

MONDAY, 28 AUGUST

A beautiful farm: ninety acres of meadow and bushland, two horses and two cows, twenty chicken and soon, we hope, more goats and lots of rabbits. We have bought a car. Imagine, our own car! John and Fred are so far the only drivers.

The house has on the main floor three rooms, one of which is being used as a bedroom, and two kitchens. One is a so-called summer kitchen, actually a closed-in verandah at the back of the house containing a stove. Having lived through a summer, I know why that is necessary. There is also a front porch. Upstairs are four bedrooms. They tell

New Haven, our very own farm, 1939

me that this is a typical Ontario farmhouse. It will be inhabited – should I say populated? – by eleven people[7] who are anything but typical Ontario farmers. No electricity, no indoor plumbing. Gerti, Mimi, and I share the largest of the upstairs bedrooms.

Our "estate" is situated about six miles from Prescott on the road to Spencerville. Every morning one of the Pollak boys will be driving us girls to the factory. At this point, most of the work falls on John. We have already had guests: the Charles Fischls, the Munks, and all the Sudeten German workers from the factory. Mounds of sandwiches – six huge platters full – were consumed in no time, washed down with buttermilk.

The European situation looks very bad. Germany made a pact with Russia, and England and France are poised for war. No word from Hans or Hella. I am very worried.

Later the same evening. Mimi and Gerti are laughing their heads off. I was reaching for the kerosene lamp, which stands (correction, stood) on the windowsill over my bed (or rather, over my mattress, for we have no beds as yet), when the cylinder landed in my lap, in pieces. What I had meant to report when I was thus rudely interrupted was that today, during our lunch break, Margaret Coburn drove up to take the four of us to a friend of hers for lunch. The kindness and attention of the Prescott people is heartwarming. Needless to say, as I was sitting to the right of the hostess, making polite conversation, there was no hint of the ache and worry within me.

Mimi and Gerti are still laughing. And I with them. Comic relief is still the best – the only – kind there is. Which reminds me: The other day a reporter was here, looking for the famous goats. When he saw that there were but fourteen of them, he asked: "How many gloves can you cut from one skin?" Told that an experienced cutter can get three gloves from a skin, he inquired (and please believe me, he was serious): "How often can you skin a goat?" Needless to say, this question has since been added to our family treasury of useful quotes.

THURSDAY, 7 SEPTEMBER

This has been a fateful week. WAR HAS BROKEN OUT. I feel sad and scared and helpless. And I used to worry when you came a little late for an appointment! Your photo on the windowsill looks at me thoughtfully, with just a trace of a whimsical smile, the same as always. How I wish I could have brought some of your manuscripts with me! Were you able to store them safely? Will I ever know?

But it's useless to ask questions into the void. Better for me to report. Life here goes on untouched by the war. Except that our pantry shelves are getting crowded with peanut butter. Peanut butter has been a recent discovery for us, a new culinary experience, and John likes it so much that he has stocked up. If war brings about rationing, as everyone is certain it will, he wants to make sure that we don't run out.

We "lovely girls" (with Gerti's and Margit's arrival, there are even more of us now) have furnished our bedroom with rugs and papered-over orange boxes. It really is quite cosy. The mattresses are covered with Persian carpets, suggesting a lush Turkish den. I have spent five dollars on an organ (someone's cast-off, of course). It sounds great except for the *vox humana* which clucks like a broody hen, and the *vox celeste* which squeaks. It has (or rather, had) an ornamental top so enormous that by dismantling it we were able to add a bookshelf, a flower stand, and a little smoking stand to our furnishings. Freddy suggested that if I allowed him to take it apart completely, he could build a racing bike.

SATURDAY, 9 SEPTEMBER

Dear me, what a celebrity I have become through the article in the Brockville *Recorder and Times!* Several days in a row, strangers have come to the office and asked to see "the educated lady." I was called out to meet them and didn't know what to say. Following a trip to Brockville, Lilly reported that the bank manager there had inquired after me; his cousin was interested in meeting me. Yesterday he appeared at the factory with his cousin, an eighty-three-year-old lady. Conversation was even more limited than on similar occasions because she was quite deaf. She looked me over carefully. I think I passed.

SUNDAY, 10 SEPTEMBER

We are expecting visitors today: the Horans (we call Mr Horan "Burgomaster," much to his amusement), and of course the inevitable Father Briceland, and the Davidsons. Yesterday we baked all afternoon in preparation for this visit and made little *koláče*,[8] two *Torten*, and two kinds of cookies.

And in Europe they are at war. I was told that mail can perhaps reach Germany via Yugoslavia. Do I dare send a greeting through Bertl Steiner?[9]

WEDNESDAY, 13 SEPTEMBER

Fateful thirteen. Will something decisive happen? Here on our farm it is incredibly peaceful. The nights are clear and starry, the crickets are putting on concerts. I can hardly believe that these meadows, these quiet cosy nooks, this bush which is turning orange and yellow and brown and crimson actually belong to us.

SUNDAY, 17 SEPTEMBER

We harvested oats today. In each sheaf that one touched, some life stirred and scampered away: grasshoppers, toads, even a little snake. It has been a hot day; I imagine the sheaves provided welcome shade. I still find it difficult to grasp that this is our soil, our life. As the toad jumped away, it made me feel that I was an intruder.

TUESDAY, 19 SEPTEMBER

Russia has invaded Poland. Poland no longer exists. What next? Here everything goes on in its peaceful way as if nothing had happened. Last Tuesday we young people were invited to the Horans, and on Thursday Mimi and I attended a "missionary circle," where

Fred and goats, 1939. "How often can you skin a goat?"

we hemmed infants' shirts. And on Sunday we were invited to the Davidsons for tea. Just before we left, we had a surprise visit by a carload of people – strangers – from Brockville, about eighteen miles from here. Just looking us over.

Lilly told me that she and Mrs Horan are conspiring to try and get me back into teaching. But I am not supposed to know about it, for my protection. I am, after all, committed to working in the factory.

John learned from Dr Smellie – the local physician, who also has befriended us – that a medical student in Brockville wants to meet him and that a university professor near Brockville expressed an interest in me.[10] Dr Smellie will introduce us. A reporter from Ottawa came to the factory to interview me. He asked about the difference in climate between here and the Old Country, whether the soil here is suitable for goats, and other similarly exciting topics. I am curious to see what appears in the paper.

Stubborn goats and novice goatherds, New Haven, 1939. *Left:* Mimi and Margit; *right:* Adolf

WEDNESDAY, 20 SEPTEMBER

Lilly gave me a lecture. She said that I am too loyal (meaning to you, Hansl) and have built a wall around myself, which one can sense. I should stop waiting, she urged. What is there to say?

One could laugh one's head off about the way the work on the farm has been apportioned. Táta – our good old Papa, but since war broke out we try to stick to Czech terms – milks the goats. Can you imagine? He is rather slow-moving, certainly much slower than the nanny goat, and much, much portlier. He tries to put her on a stool for the operation, which she doesn't accept graciously. But as the son and grandson of farmers, he comes the closest of all of us to being a real farmer. So he is the expert, while Uncle Otto is the proverbial know-it-all. Uncle Otto likes to talk; Táta is the silent type. But neither has much to say in English – it's a very foreign language for both of them. Fred claims that his father thinks that if he fractures his German he is speaking English.

Aunt Milly looks after the pigs. Aunt Milly! She used to be the elegant one, the one who could afford summer holidays at the seaside and in general was somewhat of a grande dame. Now she is the one who tackles the big sow. She does it rather well. Mutti and Aunt Antschi share the rest of the work, though Aunt Antschi is the most practical and efficient of the three. They bake bread and garden, and wield the hammer when necessary.

We four girls[11] are driven six miles to the factory every morning, either by John or Fred, stopping at the Domville cheese factory on the way to deliver the goat milk. I have been taken off the sewing machine and am now pressing the finished gloves on the special heated forms. Apart from the fact that this is a stand-up job and therefore rather tiring, it is neither difficult nor stressful. And my mind can wander – which it does, of course. Mostly backwards. Strange to be in a position where one has no idea at all of what lies ahead.

Meanwhile, daily life goes on merrily, with lots of amusing incidents. Gertsch, Mimi, John, and Fred all have a great sense of humour. The old folks seem to have lost theirs, at least for the time being. The strain of eleven people living under one roof is beginning to show. Perhaps worse than the strain of too much togetherness is the friction caused by the fact that in our farming operation the blind are leading the blind; everyone has an opinion and no one really knows for sure. Uncle Otto and Aunt Milly are the most (in fact, the only) cantankerous ones. Táta is basically peaceful and placid, though he has a strong temper when roused. Mutti and Aunt Antschi are very fond of each other, and I have never witnessed an argument or tension between them. Aunt Milly is the least intelligent and mature of the sisters; she may also be under more of a strain, with Ruth still in England, not wanting to join her mother and Margit in Canada. The consensus among the rest of us is that Ruth probably welcomes being on her own. She is staying with friends in London, a painter with a harem of four women, including one to whom he is married. Ruth had to interrupt her study of medicine and switched to chemistry.

Most of the actual farmwork falls on John and Fred. They are super sports. Fred is beginning to cope with English. After driving us to town, he has to do the shopping. He does it with zest and ingenuity and with very limited English, and in the evening he has us in stitches with tales of his adventures. Take his search for thumbtacks. After establishing the proper word for them, which was not easy, where was he to get them? Who would think of looking for them in a drugstore? In Europe, drugstores sell drugs. One day last week he had to buy a sieve for the kitchen. He didn't know the English term, but he is resourceful. "Water go, peas stay," he demonstrated and promptly received the desired article, along with a broad smile. But he says there was no smile when he asked the butcher, "Do you have any brains?" Incidentally, Canadians don't consider brains a delicacy as we do.

Fred and John, city slickers both, delight in their adventures and misadventures as farmers. Fred is a riot when he describes his efforts at ploughing – a new venture, at best – with our team of horses, quite good-looking specimens. But – and it's a big but – they have been used to drawing the milk wagon, which means that they have been trained to halt after every few steps and at the slightest provocation. Fred, as he tells it, doesn't dare make a sound, including the bodily noises in which he likes to indulge when he believes himself alone. ("With every fart, the horses stop.")

Uncle Otto and Táta went to an auction on a neighbouring farm. The owners were moving away. Auction sales seem a common phenomenon around here, a new experience for us. In Europe, one would not dream of selling everything and simply moving elsewhere. But here, just imagine the treasures that can be bought, and the temptation for such as us who are starting from scratch! And true enough, Otto and Ada [my father] returned very pleased with themselves for having made what they considered a very useful purchase. As they unloaded, we gathered around the car, somewhat puzzled.

"It's a bathtub," they explained.

We howled with laughter. It is made of tin and is rectangular with straight walls and with a divider in the middle. A milk cooler to Canadians. (It is actually proving quite useful – outdoors, as long as the days are warm – as a bathtub.)

We are learning to make do, pioneer style. No wonder our Canadian visitors consider us intriguing, with our quaint Czech ways of doing things! They seem especially interested in our goats. "Raising Kids

3 JUNE 1939 – DECEMBER 1941

around Prescott May Yet Become a Highly Lucrative Occupation" was the headline of one newspaper article. I hope the reporter is right, though somehow I doubt it. He goes on to say that these Czech farmers don't fit the image of a typical European peasant. He has a point there.

Again and again, I am singled out in these reports as "young, attractive and soft-spoken, distinctly intellectual." A summary in *Canada Weekly* of 9 September, entitled "Czechs in Canada," didn't mention names, but it started out this way:

The high quality of many of the new citizens which this country is attracting by reason of the unsettled condition of central Europe and refusal of democratic peoples to accept the yoke of German rule is demonstrated by conversation with the Czechs who are settling in Prescott and vicinity in connection with the kid-glove manufacturing industry which has been started in that town by a refugee industrialist who has transferred his business, with an established world market, to Canada. One of the young women who goes to work daily in this factory is, it has been revealed, a Doctor of Philosophy of the University of Prague who specialized in Germanic and Slav languages, with philosophy, and who taught these subjects in her native land before leaving it a few weeks ago.

Uncle Charles with his degree from the Sorbonne comes next. Mr Morgan, editor of the Brockville *Recorder and Times* sent me the clipping. "The unsettled condition of central Europe," meaning that Europe is at war – what a delicate way of putting it! Another longish article, this one in the *Ottawa Citizen*, was forwarded to me "with compliments" by R.A. Jeffery.

I am beginning to study British and Canadian history to become acquainted with our new surroundings in a wider sense. Mr Coburn helps with material. Margaret has left to start her first teaching job. How I envy her!

SUNDAY, 24 SEPTEMBER

We had twenty-six visitors today. The entire Czech population of Prescott, plus two from Brockville. One of them was Mr Koktan, a

Czech Canadian butcher, who has been here for many years and was delighted to meet some compatriots. A big talker, about forty years old. He brought along Bill Burns, a medical student, a handsome young man of twenty-two, intelligent, lots of fun. He even appreciates our brand of humour. They must have liked it here. They came at 2:30 and stayed long after everyone else had left, until 1 AM! I have a feeling that they will be back.

Rumour has it that Louis has been having problems learning to drive the car. In an effort to avoid too much public scrutiny – lets face it, everything we do is news – and embarrassed because he has to *learn* to drive while Canadians seem to be able to drive almost before they can walk, he began practising surreptitiously, without the instructor, early in the morning before Prescott wakes up. But the other day his horn stuck and he was heard, and seen, by all of Prescott as they rushed to their windows at the sound of the howling siren.

WEDNESDAY, 27 SEPTEMBER

A letter from Mr Morgan, the journalist. He is making inquiries about the possibility of my getting back to teaching.

Tension and trouble in the factory. Louis and Maña are on edge and seem petty, at times almost nasty. Especially Maña, who in turn influences Louis. I am treated civilly; it's Mimi who suffers from their black mood. But I'm sure they have worries. We get only the ripples on the surface as they affect us.

TUESDAY, 17 OCTOBER

Germany is at war, really at war. The big event here on the farm is that we now have electricity. Electric light will make a lot of difference to me, now that we don't have to crowd around one kerosene lamp. I intend to study history and French and English literature. Did I report that at the suggestion of the Horan family, our place has been named New Haven?

Have sent off another letter to Hans, via Sweden. Just as a sign of life. I couldn't really say too much. But why don't I hear from you?

Ella Fischl and daughter Mimi, New Haven, 1940

Russia allied with Germany. What a bizarre turn of events! Who now, among the other European nations, owes allegiance to whom? If it were not so deadly serious one could call it a tragicomedy.

It has been a gorgeous autumn. Those maples! Never in my life have I seen such a glorious show of multicoloured foliage, from flaming crimson to palest yellow, and all conceivable hues and shades and mixes of orange and brown. In between, white birches and dark evergreens. No two trees are alike. But within a few days all this splendour has disappeared. What's left now are the black, bare branches, some supporting huge nests that have suddenly become visible.

SUNDAY, 22 OCTOBER

It has been a relatively quiet Sunday for a change, with only Mr and Mrs Morgan from Brockville, a Slovak family from somewhere nearby, and Felix and Lilly Munk dropping in. Last Sunday we had thirty-one visitors. They seem to consider our farm to be a suitable destination for a Sunday excursion. We are amused and pleased, yes, and flattered by this

Ella (*right*) and her sister Antschi Pollak, New Haven, 1940

attention. Quite a change from being outcast as subhumans! In preparation for these Sunday invasions (for, of course, we never know how many
may drop in), the mothers bake cookies and bread and fill big platters
with *Belegte Broetchen*, which to Canadians seem exotic but are the only
kind we know: small open-faced sandwiches, holding a mix of little bits
of salami, sardine, pickle, tomato, hard-boiled egg, etc. Colourful and
tasty. The bread "we" make – Aunt Antschi, chiefly – tastes very much
like the bread at home: rye, sourdough. The spongelike Canadian white
bread is good only when toasted.

Last Friday was a concert (so-called) in church, with a performance
of Czech folksongs by the Pollak trio John, Freddy, and Gerti as the
pièce de resistance. Afterwards, during the inevitable "lunch" of tea

and cookies, just about everyone came up to us with words of welcome and something nice to say. It made us feel good.

Plans are afoot for a Czechoslovak evening, to take place tomorrow on the occasion of a visit by the Czechoslovak consul from Montreal, followed by a big reception at the Horans for all of us. And preceding this, we girls are invited for supper. In fact, Mimi and I have received two invitations; Marjorie Davidson and Mrs Burns are still fighting for the honour.

All this while there is war in Europe. I do live a life on two levels. More friction in the factory. Even Lilly has joined the other bosses in being hard on Mimi. Still, we sing folksongs all day while we work.

FRIDAY, 27 OCTOBER

How I wish I had some of your musical manuscripts! Last Wednesday afternoon, while we were at work, the Rev. Mr Coburn was here and "secretly" fixed the organ. I had mentioned to him in passing that the pedal seems to be misbehaving, making a little music go a long way; if I play in the morning, it is still playing when we return from work. It was an exaggeration of course, meant to be a joke, but he acted on it. The mothers were not supposed to mention his visit, but I noticed the improvement that very evening. Isn't he a dear? Even though Margaret is away teaching, I still spend a lot of time with the Coburns, usually during the lunch hour. They live quite close to the factory. (Who doesn't? Prescott is not exactly a metropolis.)

SATURDAY, 4 NOVEMBER

The Czechoslovak concert, consisting of a presentation of tap-dancing little girls, followed by an address by Dr Pavlásek about the CSR,[12] was a big event. The Hus words *Pravda vítězí,* [Truth will prevail], which is part of the Czech emblem, formed the theme of the talk; we were also urged to support the Red Cross. During the reception at the Horans afterwards, Father Briceland managed to squeeze some thirty of us into a picture — nineteen members of the family, plus the hosts and guests of honour (Dr Pavlásek had brought along the Polish consul general,

Mr Pawlica). How startlingly alike Táta and Uncle Louis look in the photo! They could be twins. In the flesh they don't seem that similar.

WEDNESDAY, 8 NOVEMBER

New Haven, not a bad name. Last night, the New Haven young folk (I'd better get used to it) were invited to a dance on a farm a few miles from here. The entire youth and some not so young from several miles around were assembled in a barn, and all eyes were turned on the six of us as we arrived. They were dancing round dances, which they call square dances (somewhat like our quadrilles and folk dances). The music – two violins, an accordion, and a guitar – was loud and peppy. One man called out commands in quick set phrases and in a peculiar singsong. The action was fast paced, allowing no time for reflection or translation – or mistakes! Needless to say, we messed up every "square" that we were in. Despite the hopeless confusion which we novices created, we were not allowed to learn by watching. I was sore from laughing. And it was fun seeing the variety of ages and types and shapes all frolicking together. There were about forty or fifty of us, and everyone had a good time. Now I know what is meant by a barn dance. At midnight, sandwiches, coffee, and cake appeared, and after this "lunch" we drove home.

Another invitation included the whole family, though Uncle Otto stayed behind to hold the fort. This was quite a different occasion: to the home of Senator Hardy, near Brockville. A formal tea, polite conversation. Afterwards we were shown around the estate. They have a large herd of cows. When we returned, Otto told us that in our absence two people had driven up and brought in a gramophone, which they placed on the table and proceeded to play, expectantly watching his reaction. He managed to convey to them that we were not interested in buying it, and they finally left. Despite his protestations (mostly in Czech, enhanced by appropriate gestures, I presume), they insisted on leaving a prospectus behind. They were Jehovah's Witnesses, and of course they had no intention of selling their machine.

More social activity. Following a concert in Brockville, we were invited to coffee by Mr Morgan's mother-in-law, Mrs Bowie – a very

English, very proper, very refined old lady, who could have stepped out of (or into) *Pride and Prejudice*. She had invited what seemed like the crème de la crème of Brockville society (the upper twenty-seven, so-to-speak) and made a special point of introducing me and passing me around. For once, conversation went beyond "What's the weather like in your country?" There even was a little shop talk. One guest, whose collar marked him as a reverend and whose accent I at first thought was Czech but turned out to be Scottish, asked me why I wasn't teaching. If it wasn't possible in high school, why not at a university? I told him that I was supposed to work in the glove factory and that, anyway, I wouldn't know how to go about getting a teaching position. Whereupon he pulled out his notebook, wrote down my name, and said, "Let others take care of that." His name is Dr McLeod.

On Wednesday, Uncle Louis returned from Ottawa with a surprise for me. Grinning from ear to ear, he reported that Mr Blair – the much-feared Mr Blair of the Immigration Department – had asked him if he, Louis, would agree to my giving a talk in Ottawa. I have no idea when, what, where, or how, but I am excited about it.

FRIDAY, 10 NOVEMBER

A letter from Ottawa inviting me to address the junior branch of the League of Nations Society in Ottawa on 25 November about my experiences. The Business and Professional Women's Club has invited me to speak at a luncheon on the same day.

SUNDAY, 26 NOVEMBER

Yesterday afternoon at 5:30, as I lay on Miss Ann Dewar's couch in her darkened living room, dressed in her housecoat, I was supposed to be catching ten minutes' sleep. But unable to "switch off," I was reliving the day's events. In my mind's eye, I saw Hanni, in her black dress and Lilly's fur coat (Lilly had insisted) riding to Ottawa on the bus. Canadian buses are comfortable, with padded seats. The bus arrives at the Ottawa terminal at 12 noon, on schedule. Hanni descends and looks around. An elderly lady approaches her: "Dr Fischl? I am Miss Grant."

Into the car. From this moment on, Miss Grant never stops talking
while I try in vain to contribute something to the conversation. We arrive at the Chelsea Club, an elegant building with splendid club rooms.
Up a grand staircase I am being shown to my room. Luxuriously appointed. I wash up and comb my hair. I? Is this really me? No, it's she –
Dr H.F. in her little black dress. Putting on some lipstick. Descending
to the lounge, where the ladies have been gathering. Tall ones, short
ones, fat ones, thin ones. Seventy of them. Elegantly dressed. I am the
only one without a hat.

One after the other, they are introduced to "Dr Fischl, our guest
speaker." It was supposed to have been a small, private lunch, but the demand was so great that they had to turn people away. There is only room
for seventy. Then we sit down to lunch. It looks good, but Dr F only
nibbles at her food. Finally, dessert and coffee, and then the president
rises to introduce the speaker. Dr F's heart goes put put, but after the
first few sentences she is quite relaxed. She sees some of the audience
smile. When some seem to strain and cup their ears, Dr F tries to raise
her voice.

She is supposed to be talking about Czechoslovakia. The best way of
doing this, it seems to her, is by describing her first impressions of Canada.
Life here seems so much less stressful: the rocking chairs on the verandahs
in Prescott tell a story, as does the absence of fences between people's
houses; the casual way in which people switch "jobs" (no equivalent for
that word in Europe, where everyone is committed firmly, and after
lengthy preparation, to a trade or profession). These and other little differ-
ences invite comparisons. Last but not least is the seemingly relaxed Canadian attitude about politics, which leads to an account of the stresses and
tensions in the Old Country, brought on by the rise of Hitlerism. Warm
words about our dear republic. Dr F does not use any notes. She wants her
remarks to sound casual, but she has of course carefully prepared and re-
hearsed them. Afterwards there is a "discussion" – that is to say, the
speaker is inundated with such questions as "Tell us about glove making"
… "What was the weather like in Czechoslovakia?" … "Why did you
choose Canada?"

Later, she is being driven around Ottawa and shown the main sights. She learns that although Parliament is closed to the public today, a visit has been arranged, and she is being led through the building — all very beautiful and impressive — and taken all the way up to the top of the tower. The Peace Tower it is called. She is shown an illuminated book, and the carillon is pointed out. It reminds her of the famous old one at the City Hall in Prague, where she often stood on her way from and to lectures to watch the apostles come out. Then tea at Miss Dewar's. And here she lies for ten minutes before leaving for the meeting with the League of Nations young people.

Later. It went very well. I was actually more relaxed and by then felt quite experienced. I told them the story of Czechoslovakia. Starting with legend, Přemysl and Libuše,[13] Good King Wenceslas (whom they know from Christmas carols, while we don't) — just to show how old a story it is — and then skipped a few centuries to more recent events. I talked about Prague, the "golden city" with the hundred towers, and about Masaryk;[14] and then about the marching SA[15] hordes and the Hitler threat. My ending was quite impromptu, about an experience this morning on my way to Ottawa. The sight of the bus driver in his natty grey uniform and tall boots had made my heart skip a beat with a surge of fear because he reminded me of a Nazi stormtrooper. What a relief to remember that this was a kindly, sensible Canadian bus driver! The young people seemed very interested, and their questions actually related to the things I had spoken about. No talk about the weather.

Afterwards three ladies invited me, though I am not sure to what and whether it was for then and there or for some future date; but at this point I simply smiled gratefully and followed where I was led. We had "lunch" in someone's house. Back in my room at the Chelsea Club, several letters awaited me from women who had attended the luncheon, thanking me, welcoming me, and inviting me to come back.

I was far too excited to get much sleep. In the morning, a hot bath and big breakfast revived me, and then I was picked up to be taken to church. Said to be the largest church in Canada. Again I was introduced and introduced and introduced, congratulated, welcomed, invited.

I now have six invitations to speak in Ottawa: to the League of Nations Society (adults this time), the Teachers' Institute, the Refugee Committee, a group of schoolchildren, a church group, and some women's club. Had lunch at Miss Dewar's together with Miss Roberts, who is the daughter of the Canadian poet of that name.[16] Miss Dewar tells me that she is writing a series of children's books and wants me to contribute a volume about two children travelling through Czechoslovakia; friendship and kindliness to be the theme.

MONDAY, 27 NOVEMBER, BACK IN NEW HAVEN
From the reports of the *Ottawa Citizen* and *Ottawa Journal* about our meeting, I learned that the luncheon had been arranged by Miss Muriel Kerr and Miss L. Armstrong, conveners of their international committee.

More invitations: from the WCTU (Woman's Christian Temperance Union) in Brockville, the Easton's Corners United Church, and the Maynard United Church; and I spoke in Prescott at St Paul's United Young People's group. The account of it in the local paper was headlined "Noted Czech Girl Speaks at YPU" and said, "She held the rapt attention of a large group of young folk through an interesting and humorous comparison of living conditions and tribal customs as between the Old World and the New." I had described the various festivities, customs, and special holidays.

CHRISTMAS EVE
Since we have no money for extras, we have declared a moratorium: absolutely no presents. But we did cut a tree in our bush, decorating it the way we have always done, with lanterns of coloured tissue paper, paper chains, silver-covered walnuts fastened with toothpicks, and pine cones. We baked the thread into the meringue *Pusserln* [little kisses] so that they could be hung on the tree, and made other Christmas cookies. With the oranges and apples, the tree looks nice. Most of it edible.

And then Mr Koktan arrived. To our consternation, he proceeded to unload his bag, filled with presents for us all, which he then placed under the tree. We quickly convened a council of war. We had to get him some presents, naturally. But would he not be embarrassed if nobody else received anything from anyone? Our solution was brilliant and lots of fun: each of us would find some of our own things that looked reasonably new to be wrapped and labelled.

Bescherung[17] turned into quite a performance, and Mr Koktan must have been puzzled by the extraordinary hilarity which some quite ordinary presents elicited – sober items such as socks and underpants and jars of peanut butter (of which John received several). On the other hand, we all got into the act and produced some real surprises. The mix of responses, some faked, some genuine, together with the seeming incongruity of cause and response in general and with Mr Koktan's innocent perspective made for the most unusual Christmas Eve we ever had. We were all bursting with suppressed laughter, and when we had a legitimate chance to laugh, the hilarity seemed quite out of proportion to the cause.

CHRISTMAS DAY

Your name's day. Congratulations, wherever you are.

I have met some interesting people: Wilson MacDonald, a Canadian poet who currently lives in Prescott, invited me to supper and, a few days later, to a large party. Besides writing poetry, he is a composer, he draws, cooks (invents recipes), and knows magicians' tricks. What he does best, however, is poetry. I like the sound of some of his verse:

> Lord of the mountains, dark with pine,
> Lord of the fields of smoking snow ...

The party was a bandit hunt in the sandhills halfway between Prescott and Domville. Early afternoon, some thirty of us assembled at the MacDonalds and from there were driven to the woods, where Mr MacDonald, the bandit, was hiding. Three people were assigned to act as his guards, while the others were divided into three groups and spread out for the search. The prize for finding and capturing the bandit was a volume of his poetry. Mr MacDonald had disguised himself as a woodcutter and was actually passed, unrecognized, by one group while he really was cutting down a tree. Afterwards we all met again at the Coburns for beans, bread and butter, and coffee. (They called them "baked beans" – apparently another Canadian institution.) Then, while most of us sat on the floor, the lights were dimmed and Mr MacDonald recited his poems. I was the only "newcomer" – the others were all established Prescott folk.

21 JANUARY 1940

When Wilson MacDonald heard that his friend, the principal of a boys' school in Port Hope, was looking for a secretary, he suggested my name, and I was asked to come for an interview. The principal of Trinity College met me at the station: a very friendly, pleasant man. Walking through the schoolyard with all the young people milling about gave me the strangest feeling, and at the thought of working with them I felt my throat constricting. We went to his office, where we were joined by two men (who I assume were teachers) and I was dictated a letter, which I then had to type. Obviously I did not pass the test – I type with three fingers – but they were very kind. I was taken to lunch at the residence and met Mrs Principal and their five young children, and at the end of the day they offered me the position of governess, to work for them privately. I told them that I really appreciate their confidence, but that I cannot in good conscience accept this offer: unless I find a position directly associated with a school, I don't feel justified in deserting the factory. (What I didn't also say was that I really don't want to be nursemaid/nanny to five children.)

22 JANUARY

The first of January was our tenth anniversary. I sent you a greeting via the States and Yugoslavia, with a U.S. return address. I also wrote to Hella. Why don't I hear from either of you? The silence is frightening. And ominous.

Wilson MacDonald's party was written up in the paper as a special event. It was followed by many other festive gatherings, though none quite as spectacular, to which we were invited. Christmas seems to be the season for partying. One day after Christmas, Mrs Hardy (wife of the senator and, according to Mrs Coburn, daughter of the millionaire Fulford) called on us and brought us a radio. A thoughtful, generous gift. I was delighted last night to be able to listen to Brahms' Variations on a Theme by Haydn. It reminded me of your doctoral dissertation on the orchestral *Klangbild*[18] in Brahms. I wonder if you are able to work.

I am preparing my talk for Ottawa, which is coming up a week from today.

30 JANUARY

Last Saturday was the big day. First I spoke at the Zonta Club (another professional women's club) at the Chateau Laurier. According to the reports in the Ottawa *Citizen* and *Journal*, the occasion was "a special luncheon" (presumably in contrast to the regularly scheduled meetings) and the speaker "dealt with highlights in the history of her country, its conquest by the Nazis, and some of her personal experiences. Miss Ida Cummings presided, and Dr Fischl was introduced by Mrs H.C. Cooke." The report went on to detail some of the points I made about Masaryk, about our rather progressive social institutions, about our university, the oldest in central Europe, about Prague, the historic, picturesque capital, about the growing political tension after Hitler's rise to power in Germany, about my "escape" to England, and finally about my (or rather, our) present activities. It pointed out that I have mastered English in less than a year and that it is now my ambition "to fit myself for the teaching profession in Ontario."

Mrs Cooke[19] had picked me up at the bus terminal and taken me to her home. They live on Riverside Drive, a prestigious part of old Ottawa, and for the next two days I was surrounded by elegant grandeur and comfort. The bus had arrived at noon, as before, and the luncheon was to begin at 1:15. Mrs Cooke first of all made me eat something so that I wouldn't have to eat immediately before my talk, and then we chatted until it was time to leave for the Château Laurier. They had set up a large T-shaped table, with the guest speaker enthroned at the centre of the T. The lunch looked tempting, but of course I didn't touch it, which seemed to disturb the waiter who hovered near me and finally inquired whether I would like a glass of milk.

It really was a big success. A triumph of sorts, according to Mrs Cooke, who said, "Within forty minutes you won Ottawa over for yourself and the refugees."

"First rate specimen," I heard someone behind me say. Afterwards they came up to me one by one (there were again some seventy or so women there, although the club has only thirty-five members), each more extravagant in her compliments than the other. Again I was the only hatless one; also by far the youngest.

Later I was taken to the radio station (in the building) for a microphone test. I am to be involved in a broadcast in the near future. Tea at the YWCA at 4 PM, where I met more people and gave my speech again. This one went even better; I was more relaxed. Afterwards, as before, compliments, invitations, pleasantries. We arrived back at the Cookes at 6:30. I am allowed to lie down for an hour (far too revved up to think of sleep) and at 7:45 PM we are off again, to dinner with Mr and Mrs Jenness. He is, I believe, the director of the National Museum.[20] Widely travelled; they have been to Europe several times. On the piano is music by Bach, Beethoven, Schubert, Schumann, Kramer. Mrs Cooke tells me that half of Ottawa is trying to find me a position in the civil service so that I can live in the city.

And now I am back at New Haven, in our room which we have dubbed "the iceberg." Or is it *Eisburg*? [ice castle]. Great hilarity: Mimi's comb has acquired an interesting twist while left lying on the radiator in the living room. Which prompted Sist (who, as we all know, is self-conscious about the hint of O in her legs) to ask Mutti whether she had perhaps been placed on a heater when she was a baby.

A nice letter arrived today from Athens (Ontario!), where I am to speak on 26 February. But before that I am performing in Brockville (13 February) and in the Chelsea Club, Ottawa (17 February). I am beginning to move around like the Salvation Army.

Skiing on the Prescott sandhills, 1940. *Left to right:* Hanna, Gerti, Margit, Mimi

31 JANUARY

A letter arrived from Senator Cairine Wilson who, the Coburns tell me, is the first and only woman senator and a person of considerable influence in Canadian public life. She regrets not having met me last Sunday, but apparently her daughter heard my talk and "was delighted" with it. She asks about John Pollak's studies (I had mentioned to Mrs Cooke that he had to break off his medical studies in Prague) and says she is coming to Prescott next Tuesday.

Since the last rather heavy snowfall, we have been out on skis several times. Did I report that last September a huge wooden container arrived with some of our belongings: furniture, linen, dishes, etc., including our skis? What's missing are proper hills. The only perceptible elevations far and wide are the sandhills between our farm and Prescott. I don't know how much, if any, skiing was done around here before we came, but at the moment it is a popular activity, with several novices taking it up. Last week, the Prescott Ski Club was founded, and the town of Prescott decided to help matters along by dumping some additional sand on our minuscule hills. We'll change Canada's contours yet!

I have had a full weekend: worked on a new talk, went skiing twice, washed thirteen pairs of stockings, and read Priestley's *Let the People Sing*. Pleasant reading.

WEDNESDAY

Yesterday, Senator Cairine Wilson and Mrs Anna Cooke came to town. After visiting the factory, we had lunch at the Fischls,[21] and afterwards they called on the Bäumls, who also belong to our Czechoslovak colony. Cairine Wilson is a tall, slim woman, soft spoken, caring (what's in a name?). If I didn't know she was politically active, I would almost call her shy. Maña carried much of the conversation. I was content to be a listener. At one point, Mrs Cooke took me aside to suggest that it might be better if I didn't look around for another position just yet. By not adhering to the terms of my permit, she said, I could spoil the chances of other prospective immigrants. My disappointment lasted only a few seconds. Of course she is right.

Another Ottawa visit in the offing: Miss Muriel Kerr has invited me for the weekend, to a teachers' convention. It will be nice just to sit back and listen to others for a change. I am looking forward to it. And Mr Coburn told me that he has had three inquiries, from Brockville, Athens, and Smiths Falls, asking under what conditions Miss Fischl would speak to them. Conditions? It hadn't occurred to me that there might be any, apart from the fact that someone has to drive me.

THURSDAY

Some Canadian tribal customs and favourite topics of conversation:

1 The weather. While we were brought up to consider talk about the weather a no-no (proof of having nothing better worth saying), here it is not only acceptable, it is a great opener: "Nice morning!" "Nice day!" "What do you think of the winter?" Or, on a more academic

plane, "How does the Canadian climate compare with the climate in Czechoslovakia?" But let's face it, they have so much more of it than we ever had.

2 "How do you like this country?" "I love it!" (Who would dare say anything else even if it were not so?) "Not a bad country, eh?" (Response as above.)

3 Canadians move at a more leisurely pace. I have yet to see anyone run. They don't even like to walk. Mr Elliott, the Fischls' landlord, who lives just round the corner, always visits them by car. I watched a man drive into a ditch. He didn't even bother to get out of the car to see how to extricate himself – which, I must confess, he was able to do eventually.

15 FEBRUARY

What a week! First, Ottawa. I heard four interesting lectures, was a guest at a gala dinner, and was "the" guest at two tea parties which had been arranged because I was there. I was introduced to all sorts of important people, such as the presidents of various clubs, an inspector of something or other, and the mayor of Ottawa. There were actually some men among them (the inspector and the mayor, for instance). Ottawa seems to be a city of women. Much of the civil service workforce consists of women, and they have to stay single if they want to keep their government jobs.

About twenty-five ladies were invited to the Sunday tea at which I was the centrepiece. I was by far the youngest. They deposited me in the best chair and took turns occupying the seats on either side of me. Each new neighbour tried to be original in phrasing her inquiry: How about the weather in the CSR compared with the Canadian climate? And without fail, as soon as we had dealt with topic 1 and started on topic 2 (How do you like Canada?), it was time for musical chairs again.

But I shouldn't laugh. They were very kind. What sort of profound conversation is possible in the circumstances? The funny ritual was actually imposed by my own rigid schedule. I had to make the five o'clock bus to Prescott. (Another item for my list of Canadiana: the once-a-day train between Prescott and Ottawa does not run on Sundays.)

Then, on Tuesday, the Brockville "concert." The room was packed (four hundred people, according to the newspaper account, an unusually large crowd), and judging from the response it was a resounding success. My talk had been preceded by slides that Mr Fulford had taken some years earlier during a tour of Europe (Austria and Denmark, nothing to do with Czechoslovakia, but when you live across the big water, Europe is Europe). It was followed by a musical program of "vocal solos" and cornet pieces and by some readings. Quite a potpourri, with my address billed as the main attraction. The aftermath was more invitations – to speak in Smiths Falls on 14 March, in Kemptville at the beginning of April, and at the Rotary Club, Wall Street United Church, and Trinity Church, all in Brockville. More delegations appeared in the factory today, with invitations to address St Peter's in Brockville on 4 March and a supper meeting in Lansdowne on 18 March.

I am beginning to get weary. Tired of my voice and of staying up late into the night, of trying to make small talk, of returning home after midnight and then having to get up to work in the factory. If they at least paid me!

2 MARCH

The press reports are beginning to fill my scrapbook. Among others:

Plans for an intensive drive for funds are now being completed by the Ottawa Refugee Committee. The government's permission to bring 100 refugee children into Canada has been received. It is understood that if the settlement of the 100 is successful, the gate will be opened wider. Senator Cairine Wilson, president of the National Committee, and Dr. Hanna Fischl, a refugee now resident at Prescott, will open the campaign by a radio broadcast tomorrow over CBO. Senator Wilson will introduce Dr. Fischl, who will be interviewed on her impressions of Canada by Bob Anderson of CBC staff. A further broadcast will be staged by Mayor Stanley Lewis of Ottawa and Mayor Horan of Prescott at 7 PM next Thursday.[22]

I can hardly keep up with events. At a banquet in Ottawa to which I was invited I found myself placed at the head table as a guest of honour. The next day was my address at the Chelsea Club. After the talk, Mrs Thomas handed me an envelope, not to be opened until I got home (which was 25 February, Mutti's fiftieth birthday; they knew this because I had told them why I could not stay over another day). As an honorarium, I received fifteen dollars from the club. As well, Mrs Davies gave me a hand-me-down fur coat. Brown pony. Thus richly laden, I returned to Prescott. The boys picked me up at the Fischls and we went skiing. There, Bill Burns (the medical student whom Mr Koktan had introduced some weeks before) and three of his colleagues appeared, on their way to our place, and we all drove home, to be joined a little later by the Munks and Fischls, who brought a table lamp for Mutti. The envelope contained a hundred dollars! A veritable fortune.

In Europe spring flowers will soon be out. Hitler seems to be planning something. I am terribly worried.

7 MARCH

A ladybug came crawling across today and rested on one of the gloves. Is it a symbol? There are rumours about peace moves in Finland.

The Brockville meeting (which was well attended, by a male audience this time, and very well received) happened to coincide with the first anniversary of my leaving Czecholovakia. Hard to believe that only a year has passed.

17 MARCH

Mimi is twenty today. Invitations for speaking engagements are still pouring in. I didn't know that Ontario has so many communities, organizations, clubs, and churches needing speakers. I will not bore you with any more of this. No, I am not getting a swollen head. Much of it is just plain funny. Take, for instance, the variation which the trip to Smiths Falls added to my experiences. (It's the last one I intend to record here.)

I took the bus to Brockville, and there I changed to a little yellow mail bus which made me feel like a postilion of bygone days. The driver, who evidently had orders to bring me, asked for me even before I boarded. It was a cold, snowy, blustery day. We stopped at every farm, depositing papers and letters and parcels in mail boxes that are impaled on poles and look like birdhouses. Along the way he presented me with a pink sweet pea, which he must have purloined from a bouquet that he was delivering. In Smiths Falls, he handed me over to my hosts, personally, of course; I fully expected him to ask them for a signed receipt.

WEDNESDAY, 27 MARCH

The Canadian winter caught up with us after all. A blizzard last Thursday buried our road in a metre of snow. Impossible to get out. We were not sorry to miss a morning in the factory. Since it was Good Friday, it would have been only half a day anyway. By Saturday morning, the sun was shining brilliantly; a glorious, glistening day. So I rode with Fred in our two-seater cutter as far as Domville to deliver the milk to the cheese factory. It so happened that a Domville farmer was driving to Prescott. (The road from Prescott via Domville to Roebuck was ploughed.) Since I wanted to ask for mail and also needed embroidery cotton for a tablecloth I am making for Mrs Coburn, I accepted his offer of a ride. After my errands, I spent most the day with the Coburns and at 5 PM returned with the farmer as arranged.

Fred was to meet me with the cutter at the Domville corner. However, the winter was not over yet. During the day, the storm had started up again and the car barely made it through the drifts. In fact, it didn't − at least not as far as the spot where I was to be met by Fred. So Hanni had to wade knee-deep (or higher) through the snow and finally, well past the appointed time, made it to the rendezvous. But far and wide, no cutter. So I trudged on. It was a bit scary, with the roadside fences drifted over and the ditches filled in. I was glad I was wearing my ski boots and pants. Suddenly, in the distance, a human figure emerged. Dear Friedl! Even the horses had not been able to make it through the drifts, so he had come to meet me on foot.

* * *

25 MAY

Almost two months have elapsed. The Germans have occupied Holland and Belgium, and have marched into Norway. People here barely take note of the war. From time to time someone will say, "Things aren't too good" (Hitler is at the Channel), but I have also heard some remark that the Allies have deliberately allowed Hitler to advance so far into France in order to be able to cut off his lines of supply.

I have given three or four lectures a week while also working nine hours a day in the factory. From now on, I am not accepting any more invitations. This is a holiday weekend (Queen Victoria's birthday) and the factory is closed for three days.

A rumour is said to be circulating in Prescott that we are German spies.

Much hustle and bustle last Saturday when forty members of the Ottawa branch of the Women's Canadian Historical Society visited our farm. As the newspaper write-up put it, "Tea was served at the home of Dr Hanna Fischl ..." (Will the rest of our clan start hating me for getting all the attention? Run me out of town as a German spy? Actually, they think it a good joke.) Yes, we did serve tea and coffee, plus sandwiches, *koláče*, and cookies, and we showed them the handicrafts, handmade carpets, etc. They paid us fifteen dollars.

Tomorrow we six young folk go on an all-day fishing trip.

11 JUNE

Hitler's armies are before Paris. Italy has entered the war. There have been terrible battles on the Western Front. Hansi, where are you? I have the feeling that by thinking of you I can keep you safe. Mimi helped by telling me that she dreamed she met you on the street in Prescott.

17 JUNE

The worst has happened: France has surrendered. At least the murder has ended. But the future looks bleak. In fact, hopeless.

30 JUNE

Visitors from Ottawa: a Mr Bowman who is editor of the *Ottawa Citizen*, and his secretary, Miss Elsie Herwig. They have been here several times now. He seems genuinely interested in everything we are doing. Once he brought us some tomato seedlings. Thank goodness, they are thriving! Not everything we try has worked out. Take, for instance, our white rabbits. We had placed great hopes in our rabbit-breeding project. It seemed a brilliant idea. Aren't rabbits proverbially fertile? We would sell the meat as well as the fur; and green food is plentiful. Why had nobody thought of it before? We built hutches and acquired some nice rabbits, making sure that both sexes were represented. They mated according to plan and produced respectable litters, but a few days later all the young were dead. The rabbit mothers had killed them. We tried again, with the same result and still don't know what has gone wrong. Someone suggested that we didn't give them enough privacy. Could this really be the case? There had, in fact, been a rather hyperbolic birth notice in the local weekly *Prescott Journal*:

First Litter Arrives – There is joy throughout the Czechoslovakian colony near Prescott over the arrival at one of the farms, "New Haven," of the first litter born to the large white rabbits which were acquired some weeks ago. The rabbits are being raised for the sale of both fur and meat in the Montreal market.

Unfortunately, they forgot to inform the rabbits what was expected of them.

And Fred still doesn't like being reminded of his misadventure with the pig. At a family council we had decided it was time to have some piglets, so Fred had loaded the sow onto the trailer and driven to a farmer who was known to own a boar.

"Is she in heat?" the farmer asked when nothing much seemed to be happening in the pig pen.

"What do you mean?" Fred asked.

"Well, you know, is she red?"

"Red where?"

"Not on the nose, of course."

That's when Fred, who is basically a city slicker but knows the facts of life, realized that the timing of the event was not for us to decide at a family council. His face by then was as red as the sow's behind should have been, and he departed with his load. Reflecting on his defeat, he got madder by the minute, and by the time he rounded the gate to New Haven, his rage made him take the corner too fast. The cart upset, and the sow took off. Have you ever tried to catch a pig? We all got into the act, and eventually we did succeed.

So that's why we are very happy to be able to report to Mr Bowman that his tomatoes are doing very well, thank you!

SATURDAY, 13 JULY

A lazy afternoon in the hot July sun. Have had a letter from Hilda Cunnington asking me to find a home here for the boys. What it must have cost them to make this decision! I feel for them. At the same time, I am proud of their confidence in me. Of course I wired at once: "Send children immediately. Don't worry. Happy to take care of them till proper home found." In the meantime, I have found one, with the help of the Coburns, of course. Mr and Mrs W.E. Crateau would love to act as their foster parents. He is editor of the local paper. They have no children of their own, are comfortably off, have a nice home in Prescott, are a warm, intelligent couple, and have been highly recommended by the Coburns. My cable said, "Family W.E. Crateau offers affectionate comfortable home. Best wishes for happy sailing." I spent the week arranging things: cables, letters, photographs, several visits with the Crateaus. I hope Michael and Nigel can actually come.[23]

I bought a piano. The harmonium is not working properly after all. Mimi asked me today to read her some Goethe poems.[24] I read "An

CANADIAN PACIFIC TELEGRAPHS

DIRECT CONNECTIONS WITH
POSTAL TELEGRAPHS - COMMERCIAL CABLES
IMPERIAL CABLES - CANADIAN MARCONI

MONEY TRANSFERRED
BY TELEGRAPH

C.D. 1M
This is a full-rate Telegram or Cablegram unless otherwise indicated by signal in the check or in the address.

TELEGRAM	CABLEGRAM		
FULL RATE	FULL RATE		
DAY LETTER	DL	CODE	CDE
NIGHT LETTER	NL	DEFERRED	LC
NIGHT TELEGRAM	NM	NIGHT CABLE LETTER	NLT

W. D. NEIL, GENERAL MANAGER OF COMMUNICATIONS, MONTREAL.

STANDARD TIME

RA AS 12 GLT VIA MARCONI CENSORSHIP

SHEFFIELD 21

DOCTOR FISCHL

PRESCOTT ONT.

LOVING REMEMBRANCES ASHDELL WINDOWLESS CHILDREN HOME CHEERFULLY

UNDAUNTED.

2 18PM   CUNNINGTON.

Cable from the Cunningtons after Sheffield had been blitzed

Schwager Kronos" and "Gesang der Geister über den Wassern." Does it seem a strange request? Not really. We feel the need to maintain some connection with the past. Everything is so different here and seems shallow. Only *seems*, I realize, because we find nothing below the surface. Perhaps we don't yet know how to reach beyond the smiling, friendly façades.

SATURDAY, 20 JULY

It is pouring with rain. I played the piano all afternoon. So far, no objections from the others.

Most of the pieces brought back memories. The *Vogelweide Lieder,* the only ones I could bring, and "Beauty," after a text by Masefield. Remember when you wrote those? The future already looked pretty grey then, and you had begun to think in terms of English texts. I also played the *Adagio* by Beethoven and the Bach *I Inventions.* The first time I played them for you, you said that you could hear the elves and gnomes of my childhood.

2 SEPTEMBER

Labour Day, the equivalent of our 1 May at home? Except that the May celebrations in the Old Country are more political. Here it is mainly a holiday.

I finished reading *The Patriot* by Pearl Buck. I devoured it in a day and a half, and afterwards I felt a great stillness within me – or perhaps I should say emptiness – as always when one has been totally immersed in an experience that suddenly is over. Now I hear the birds and the crickets again, and notice that the summer is taking its leave.

The war above England is raging with terrible fury. Does Hansi still think of me? Is he waiting for peace as I am? I shall try once more to write to Hella. The other day Mimi told me that I called Hans in my sleep. I didn't even know that I had dreamed of him. This only confirms what I have been feeling all along, that I have been living on different levels whether I knew it or not. Half of me (should I say the "outer half"?) is more active and busy than ever – did I report that I have learned to drive the car? – while the other half (the self within?) is just marking time, waiting things out, keeping still. I feel that this is a time of transition, of preparation, of getting ready – but for what? What does the future hold? Or is this it?

Yes, I have got my driver's licence. Unfortunately it is no use to me at the moment. Freddy had an accident with the car and we wonder whether the old Dodge is even worth fixing. Poor Freddy. He wasn't hurt, thank God, but his ego is very bruised and his pocketbook is affected as well. Of course we girls are chipping in to pay for the repairs.

Mimi is calling. We want to go out on our bikes. Have discovered a new road.

* * *

7 JANUARY 1941, ELMWOOD SCHOOL, ROCKCLIFFE PARK, OTTAWA

Here I am – in Elmwood! In a cosy little room, decorated in white and pink and blue. Four hours ago I moved in to join the staff of this private school for the daughters of the wealthy and powerful.

Yes, it's quite a leap in my life. Let me catch up. A month or so ago I gave myself a push, because I thought it was high time I took a serious look to see "what gives" in the teaching profession for someone like me. With Louis' permission, I hopped on the train to Ottawa and, as a start,

OFFICE OF THE
DIRECTOR

CANADA

DEPARTMENT
OF
MINES AND RESOURCES

IMMIGRATION
BRANCH

OTTAWA, 28th December, 1940.

Dear Mr. Fischl,

    I have been talking with Mrs. Buck of Elmwood School about the offer of the position made to Dr. Hanna Fischl. Senator Wilson also telephoned me yesterday before my talk with Mrs. Buck. I find that it was Senator Wilson who brought the case to Mrs. Buck's attention. When I explained our fears that these good-hearted offers are in danger of interfering with the development of a new industry, Mrs. Buck saw at once as did also Senator Wilson, the need of great care in removing skilled workers while a business is in process of becoming established.

    The proposal I have made with which Mrs. Buck is in entire agreement is that Dr. Fischl should remain with you until early next autumn when if you are agreeable to letting her go she could then seek other employment such as teaching. Mrs. Buck says that if there is still an opening at that time she will be glad to do anything possible for Dr. Fischl. I wish you would let me know whether this arrangement is acceptable at your end.

               Yours very truly,

               F.C. Blair
               Director.

Louis Fischl, Esq.,
Prescott,
Ont.

Letter to Uncle Louis from F.C. Blair, Director of Immigration, Department of Mines and Resources, Ottawa

DEPARTMENT
OF
MINES AND RESOURCES

Ottawa, 3rd January,1941.

Dear Dr. Fischl,

Our records show that you were admitted to
Canada as part of the glove industry to be established by
Mr. Louis Fischl. I understand that you are not content
to remain there and are anxious to take employment offered
you by the Principal of Elmwood School, Rockcliffe. After
talking matters over with Mr. Fischl we have agreed as a
special case to allow you to leave your work at Prescott.

It must be distinctly understood that in
taking this new work you must not do anything to take other
members of the staff away from the Prescott business. I
should like to have your undertaking to observe this
condition. If you give me this assurance in writing then
you may come to Ottawa immediately. I am sure you will
understand why we are very anxious not to do anything to
interfere with the establishment in this country of the
business in which your uncle is now engaged and it is because
of this that we have hesitated so long in agreeing to your
leaving Prescott.

Yours very truly,

Director

Dr. Hanna Fischl,
c/o Mr. Louis Fischl,
PRESCOTT,
Ontario.

Letter to Hanna from F.C. Blair

dropped in on Mr Bowman in his *Citizen* office. Had he any advice for me? Without a moment's hesitation (and certainly without any explanatory comment), he picked up the phone and dialled a number. Only when he asked to speak to Senator Wilson did I realize what was on his mind. A minute or two later he turned to me with the announcement, "You and I have been invited to tea."

In the Wilsons' grand Rockcliffe mansion,[25] the butler ushered us into the most enormous living room I have ever seen, where we were graciously welcomed by Cairine Wilson. Moments later, a middle-aged lady arrived, sporting a hat, white gloves, and a wall-to-wall smile, obviously flattered and excited to have been asked to tea by her illustrious hostess. She was introduced as Mrs Buck, principal of Elmwood School. Mrs Wilson thanked her for coming at a moment's notice. There I sat, hatless of course, practically nailed to my chair because children were crawling all over me. (I don't know whether any of them were Mrs Wilson's; I think her own five or six are all grown up. Mostly they seemed to be British evacuees.) Meanwhile, there was pleasant conversation about sweet nothings, accompanied by sweets from the tea trolley. Hardly any mention of my former career or qualifications. It is mid-term, no time to hire teachers. Still, I had indulged in a quiet hope for next fall. Well, another hope dashed, not for the first time and not for the last either.

But imagine my surprise when, two days later, back in Prescott, the mail brought a letter from Mrs Buck. There was no vacancy at this point for a teacher, she said, but would I like to join the staff to assist the matron, Mrs Elliott? Would I not! But it was not quite that simple. The Immigration Department at first refused to release the expert (!) from her commitment to Fischl Gloves. We were caught: Uncle Louis had procured our permits stating that he urgently needed us, so how could we now tell them that the company could easily survive without my services? From one day to the next my hopes alternately soared and plummeted, depending on the latest communiqué from Ottawa. In the end, Mr Blair wrote me a personal letter, granting his permission on condition that it would not be considered a precedent and that I would promise not to lure anyone else away.[26] So here I am. At the bus stop I was met by two Elmwood girls in their short green tunics: Nancy Bowman[27] and a friend. They helped load my luggage and skis onto their car and then dropped me off at her father's office while taking my belongings to the school. I spent the afternoon with Elsie Herwig[28] in the *Citizen*. Later, Nancy returned with another friend. When she introduced me as the new teacher, her friend exclaimed: "For heaven's sake!" I don't know quite how to interpret that.

Elmwood School, surrounded by a large garden, has a rather attractive, welcoming exterior, more like an oversized villa than an institution. The girls handed me over to a woman in nurse's uniform, who turned out to be Mrs Elliott. She took me on a tour. The bedrooms are all bright and cheerful, white furniture everywhere, airy curtains, colourful chintzy slipcovers. The downstairs hall is a big formal room: Persian carpets, deep club chairs, heavy drapes, exuding an air of stuffy elegance. A touch of England? The teachers' common room also has armchairs, a radio, carpets – what a world away from our *Konferenzzimmer* [staff room] in Komotau or Olmütz! My own room is part of the infirmary wing, with bathroom next door, to be shared only with Mrs Elliott. The windows look southeast, onto trees and villas. Since this is the last day of the Christmas vacation, the building is uninhabited at the moment. It will be a different story tomorrow when the boarders – about seventy-five of them – return. In addition, there are at least as many day girls, who attend classes but commute from their homes in Ottawa. (Nancy Bowman is a day girl, living in Rockcliffe, actually very near the school.) Ages range from kindergarten to senior matric.

ELMWOOD, DAY 2

At 8 AM a bell reminded us to get out of bed, and at 8:30 another one called us to breakfast. The boarders are arriving today and will be met at their respective trains, each teacher having been assigned a list of names. I am not involved in this operation, of course. But I have met seven of the teachers, those who live in the school. There are also some who live in town. With the exception of Mlle Juge, the French instructress, they are all quite young. I have yet to encounter Mrs Buck, who is said to be sick, but rumour has it that she will come today. She lives in her own house next door. I am curious what duties she will assign me.

9 JANUARY

Yesterday afternoon, with nothing to do, I went into town on some errands. At 4 PM I was to call on Elsie Herwig for a cup of tea but happened to run into Mrs Bowman, who invited me to her place. I had just returned when the call came to present myself to Mrs Buck. At her home. I shall be teaching Latin, French for the tiny tots, an extra course in German authors, and handicrafts. I am to accompany the morning hymn on the piano and play for the dancing classes. And I am to assist the matron-nurse.

Three of my classes started today: Latin (three girls!), English composition, and Mrs Buck's current events class. She is still not quite well and suggested I tell them about Czechoslovakia. Afterwards, Miss Sinden told me that the girls had talked about it at lunchtime.

Last night's *Citizen* carried a notice that Miss Hanna Fischl, PH D, etc., etc., "is this week joining the staff of Elmwood School for Girls," etc. My new colleagues pointed it out to me. This morning, a reporter from the other Ottawa paper, the *Journal*, came to the school to interview me. He didn't seem very bright and I am a little worried what he will come up with.

10 JANUARY

I had reason to be worried. What a garbled account! "Glove-making was nothing new to me. I learned to make them when I was a little girl." And "I used to attend hockey games in Czechoslovakia." What nonsense! I had never heard of hockey. "Dr. Fischl doesn't look like what you might expect a doctor of philosophy to look like. She is a very attractive, blond young woman, not too tall – and has a charming smile." Now that's more like it!

Bells, bells, bells. The days are divided into segments separated by bells: 7 AM bell to wake you; 7:30, time to get up; 7.50, first call for breakfast (for the girls); 7:55, second call for breakfast (for the teachers, though we all eat breakfast together). Then we return to our rooms to make our beds. At 9 AM the bell calls us to morning assembly (hymn and prayer). Bells between classes, bells for lunch (again, first and second call), then back to classes. The 3:30 bell signals the end of classes and time to go for a walk. The girls are not allowed to leave the house without permission. From 4 to 5 PM is study time, announced, of course, by the bell. I have not quite grasped everything. For instance, a bell just went ...

If this life were depicted in a teen novel, I would think it an exaggeration. I am told that the girls are so docile that they don't even try to play tricks. We shall see. The green tunics and white blouses uniformly cover all kinds of sizes and shapes – rather nice. For supper, civilian dress is allowed. There is a head girl, a very prestigious position, and her officers are called prefects. They help ensure that the house rules are observed and somehow form a liaison between faculty and students. Sue Kenny, the current head girl, is a dear. As are many of the others, especially the seniors.

Students come to Elmwood from near and far – from New York, Washington, Winnipeg, England – yes, and some even from Ottawa. All are daughters of the rich and prominent. But any display of affluence or even of individuality is taboo. Each girl is allowed to bring three dresses, in brown or green, six changes of underwear, and two pairs of shoes. No jewellery.

Today we go skiing. Thirty girls and three teachers. When a third escort was needed for this outing, they were relieved to discover that I have skis. And I am happy to have been discovered. I am really looking forward to this. The bus will pick us up at 10:30 and take us to Kingsmere in the Gatineau.

Last night, two girls came to my room with a tin of something. Could I translate the directions? The directions turned out to be in Norwegian, just as foreign to me as to them. But since the stuff looked like shoe polish and smelled like shoe polish, I was able to "translate." Which seems to have confirmed their belief that I understand anything "foreign." I have been able to help out in other ways as well. Miss Cumner was in despair because she had to produce a typed version of her exam questions but cannot type. Of course I offered. Miss Sinden had some trouble with the stockings she was knitting for the Red Cross. Could I help? Add to this the skiing and the fact that there is apparently nobody else to play the piano for the morning assembly, the kindergarten, and the dancing classes, and my schedule is pleasantly varied. Have I reported that in addition to Latin, German, French, and sewing, I have now been asked to teach geography and art history?

The other day I was asked to escort some of the girls to a concert, my first proper concert in how long? Piatigorsky. Gregor Piatigorsky on his cello is a magician. It was wonderful. There I sat in the tenth row in my white evening dress and fur coat listening to real music, yet I felt like crying. The music made me homesick.

SATURDAY, 25 JANUARY

On Tuesday I went with Elsie Herwig to a concert of the Ottawa Choral Society. The solo pianist was rather mediocre – his tempi painfully slow. I could barely contain my giggles when Elsie whispered to me, "I wish someone would stick a pitchfork into him." But on Thursday, a symphony concert with Bronislaw Huberman as soloist. Again I was escorting Elmwood girls, and what a treat to hear this superb violinist!

Friday was "free day." The term tests are over and on this day the girls are in charge. They choose their subjects and teachers, and carry on the supervision themselves. No free day for me though. But I am not complaining. I would have felt badly if it had been otherwise.

Mimi was in town over the weekend. Dear Sist. It was great to see her. If only she could get out of Prescott as well.

MONDAY

Today was the teachers' meeting. It went on forever. Each student is thoroughly discussed, with every detail being considered ad nauseam. For instance, we spent half an hour deliberating how to punish a girl who had been caught chewing gum – twice! (The crime was committed outside class.) I forget what we decided. Margaret Sinden is responsible for much of this. She is so darned earnest and humourless.

Diana Cumner – the Junior School teacher – and I went to a movie. Unlike Margaret Sinden, she is cheerful and laid back. We laughed a lot. But there was nothing funny about the movie. We saw *Night Train to Munich*, a suspense drama about espionage and counterespionage, concentration camps, etc. The few attempts at German in it gave me a queer feeling. Homesick? But not for the camps. We had supper downtown and came home around 10 PM. After my bath, I went to bed with a book about Napoleon, in preparation for class.

SUNDAY, 2 MARCH

Yesterday I had a bad day. The house was quiet with most of the students and staff away. I had finished my work and was alone with myself. And suddenly I felt unbearably anxious and lonely. The war is so horrible – Hitler seems to be advancing everywhere – and I don't see a way out. Communication with Europe is completely cut off.

But this is another day. I awoke with the morning sun stealing into my room. Once every two weeks I have a Sunday morning off, and this was it. They brought me a luxurious breakfast in bed and I enjoyed the sunshine, which followed me even into the bathtub. Then I put on a bright blouse and my yellow vest, got hold of my camera, and started out. A gorgeous, crisp winter morning. Glistening snow and ice, the sun already quite high – it is, after all, March. And perfect silence. I walked quite a long way.

A car passed with a load of young girls, and they waved: my girls from Geography 5. That brought me back to reality. Now I am back at school. In a few moments the bell will go, and this afternoon I am on duty.

SATURDAY, 22 MARCH

What a joyful day! A letter from Hella.[29] It came via Sweden. She has received my mail and has a message for me from Hans. The *Vogelweide Lieder* have been broadcast again. Above all, he is alive! (But why doesn't she enclose his letter?) I was so excited when her letter came that I started to sob uncontrollably. When I finally collected myself, I went for a walk.

6 MAY

Paris has fallen. We are all terribly upset, especially Mlle Juge, who seems inconsolable. Frightening beyond words.

21 JUNE

Hitler has declared war on Russia! Mlle Juge has persuaded me to register for the French summer course at McGill. It will be good practice for me and fun.

* * *

ELMWOOD, SEPTEMBER 1941

It feels good to be back. I enjoyed the summer course at McGill and life in Macdonald Hall. It gave my French a healthy boost. Mlle Juge was of course one of the profs. I like her a lot, and I think that this feeling is reciprocated. She is the only white-haired member of our staff, rather independent and outspoken, and very French (though I am not sure I know what I mean by that).

The rest of the summer I spent, of course, at New Haven. They are all working very hard and under pressure. And they are worried – as I am – about the terrible news from the front. Hearing Churchill gives us a lift, but all else is darkness. Freddy has enlisted and is overseas. As soon as John graduates, he will join the Medical Corps.

One of the pupils in kindergarten this term is Princess Beatrix of Holland. But there is to be no reference to princesses. Her mother, Princess Juliana, made a point of that when she talked with Miss Hamilton. Princesses are not to be mentioned, not even in fairy tales. Especially not in fairy tales. Beatrix is a round-faced, pink-cheeked, happy youngster. But althougth she doesn't stand out in any way, her presence does affect the rest of us. Whenever she is in the building (which is practically all day)

Fischl-Pollak clan with guest Elvins Spencer, who was not discouraged by this unusual welcome. *Left to right, front:* Adolf, Ella, Otto, Antschi, Gerti, Margit, Elvins; *behind:* Hanna, Mimi

one of her two bodyguards has to be around, which means that a huge Dutchman sits in our staff room, which cramps our style somewhat.

Another, much more welcome addition to our staff room is Edith Spencer, who has come to Elmwood to teach English. A lively, sparkling, beautiful young woman whom I liked at first sight. Edith hails from Alberta. As a child, she was a student here for a time when her father was a member of Parliament.[30] In the short time that we have known each other, we have spent much of our spare time together and have become friends. There is much laughter. As soon as it can be arranged, I shall take Edith home to New Haven to introduce her to the others. They will enjoy her as I do – she is a delight.

The Dutchmen asked Edith and me to go out to dinner with them. We accepted on condition that it remained a foursome. It was fun riding in a car that possibly belonged to Dutch royalty. For after-dinner drinks,

Hanna with Elvins Spencer, 1942

they took us to a home, a rather posh home to which someone from the Dutch Embassy had probably given them a key. Nobody else was around. And there, I am afraid, I did something terrible. I spilled red wine on the white broadloom. And what's worse, this must have happened after I had already consumed some, for I dismissed it with, "At least it makes a nice pattern!" We left shortly afterwards, and only next morning did the full weight of guilt hit me. I don't know whose home it was, nor do I want to. But I do know that I shall never forget the sight of that big red stain on the rug, which we dismissed so lightly at the time.

DECEMBER
I have invited Edith to New Haven for Christmas. Since her brother will be visiting her from Toronto, she will bring him too.

Epilogue

The journal ends abruptly. It fell silent after Edith brought her brother Elvins to New Haven for Christmas in 1941. Elvins and I fell in love and were married six months later.

When the war ended in 1945 and the Czechs were again in charge of their country, they decided to expel the Germans. All 3 million of them. The term "ethnic cleansing" had not yet been invented, but that is what we would call it today. The Czechs felt fully justified in their action. Had not the Sudeten Germans demanded to be joined to the Reich, chanting and roaring "Heim ins Reich" ad nauseam? Had they not called Hitler in, thus breaking up the republic? Having suffered under the so-called protectorate for six years, the Czechs felt no qualms about sending the Germans "home."

The German inhabitants of each town and village were ordered to gather at a certain place, and in long columns they were marched across the border, allowed to take with them only what belongings they could cart or carry. Thus, all the former Sudeten Germans were dispersed, the majority ending up in southern Germany. It was a grim and vengeful action, hitting the innocent along with the guilty. I have heard horror stories of this forced march. Those affected were mostly women, children, and old men. Men of military age, if still alive, may not have returned yet. The marchers were weakened by the deprivations of war, and the conditions they encountered after crossing into a defeated and bombed out Germany were utterly chaotic. But this is not the place to discuss this. Suffice it to say that in the course of time they were absorbed in the

German population, and in the end they fared much better than they would have if they had remained in their old home, which fell under communist rule. But the ultimate irony is that today Prague is overrun by German tourists and entrepreneurs, and German is the country's semi-official second language.

Meanwhile, on this side of the great water, Elvins and I were happily living in Trail, British Columbia, where he was working as a research chemist and I was busy changing diapers, having recently become a mother.

I had totally lost touch with Europe. It was seven years since I had last seen Hans, five years since I had had a letter from him or anyone else, and I had no idea who had survived or where anyone had ended up. In any case, my mind as well as my day was fully occupied with the present. In every sense, I had detached myself from the past, pulling down my personal "iron curtain."

The curtain did not lift for sixteen years, and then it happened almost by accident. Elvins had been appointed head of the Chemistry Section at the Federal Research Institute in London, Ontario, and I was teaching German language and literature at the University of Western Ontario. Soon after my arrival at Western, I discovered that one of my colleagues there, Fritz Wieden, was a nephew of the man who had owned the only hotel in Komotau. One day he brought me a copy of the *Komotauer Zeitung*, a newspaper published by the Germans who had been expelled from Komotau. By almost miraculous coincidence, that issue contained the address of my former class teacher, Dr Eduard Brix, who was compiling a file of the addresses of former students of the Komotau Gymnasium. I wrote to him at once and received a long, warm reply. Brix now lived in Frankfurt, and since Elvins and I were about to leave on a trip to Europe, we could easily visit him. There was a burning question I wanted to ask.

In Frankfurt a few days later, I learned that Hans Feiertag had perished in Russia during the siege of Stalingrad. But while he was on home leave in Vienna – his last leave, as things turned out – he had married, and there was a child, born posthumously. That was all Brix knew, except that the widow was a professional violinist, presumably living in Vienna. It seemed that luck was on our side because we had already planned to pass through Vienna. However, a search through the telephone directory there proved fruitless: no listing for Feiertag.

So that was that. From now on, the past would be even more a closed book, with no temptation to open it. And so it remained for the next twenty years. But my address was in Dr Brix's file, and this led to my being invited to Augsburg in 1987 for a grand gathering of former students. I was the only one there who had come from overseas. Some time after the Augsburg meet, a letter arrived like a bolt out of the blue. It was signed Carla Berndsen Merling, a name familiar to me. Although I had never met Carla, I knew that she had been a friend of Hans. She was writing to tell me that his widow Emma wanted to meet me.

I wrote to Emma, and in due course we met. I also met her daughter Susanna and grandson Sascha. It turned out that I had not been able to find Emma in the Viennese directory because she had moved back to her parents after receiving word that Hans was missing in action. She handed me the wooden figure which he had carved of me and for me; she claimed she had recognized me from this likeness when I stepped off the train. Its counter-

Figure of Hanna, carved by Hans Feiertag in 1937

part, representing Hans himself, she kept. I thought it very generous of her to give me the one and of course didn't tell her that in fact both belonged to me, a precious birthday gift from Hans many, many years ago. She also returned to me the white silk handkerchief with "Hanni" embroidered in one corner, which had been my gift to my *Tanzstunden* partner and which, she said, Hans had always kept with him. I still have it.

I found her a strange person, driven by phobias, idiosyncrasies, and distrust of everyone and everything – though fortunately not of me. She was most generous to me and somehow made me feel that I could do no wrong. She had never accepted that Hans was dead. Even forty-five years after the war, she still referred to him as "missing" and got cross if anyone suggested otherwise. For some time she had apparently believed the rumour (started by whom?) that Hans had been rescued from a Russian camp by a woman from North America. Now that she realized I was not hiding him, she planned, she said, to go to Russia to find him.

When I inquired about the Feiertag manuscripts, I was shocked to hear that although Emma had them all and was a musician herself, she had done nothing about them. She was sitting on them – almost literally. They were in a box under her bed in Vienna. Hans had stored them with Hans Hammer, his friend in Karlsbad, who had carried them to Germany when he was expelled, a precious part of the limited load he was allowed to take with him. Hammer had passed them on to Emma. I suggested that they should be somewhere where musicologists or musicians could have access, but Emma did not trust the Viennese. She was delighted when I suggested the Mahler-Rosé collection at the University of Western Ontario. Hans was born in the year of Gustav Mahler's death, and his music often reminded me of Mahler's, though Hans was definitely trying to find his own voice.

On my return to London, Ontario, I consulted various people in Western's Faculty of Music, as well as Bill Guthrie, who was in charge of the Music Library. They were, of course, happy to receive this donation and agreed to mark the occasion with a concert of Feiertag music, with Emma attending. Her daughter Susanna came over a month or so ahead of time with the manuscripts. Seeing the music again and recognizing in many instances my own handwriting brought a lump to my throat. I had forgotten how much of the material I had copied; there were no photocopiers in those days. As well, many of the poems that Hans set to music had been favourites of mine which I had drawn to his attention, and I had transposed the ancient *Vogelweide* verses into modern idiom for him.

The concert was produced and performed by members of the Faculty of Music. It took place one Sunday afternoon in the fall of 1987, followed by a reception. Many of our friends attended; and our family, of course, including grandchildren Hilary and Gregory. Sister Mimi even came from Vancouver. Dr Jeffrey Stokes, who had just taken over as dean of music, was surprised that the audience all but filled the recital hall.

Since then, Elvins and I have visited Austria on several occasions. We met Emma each time, and we also became friends with Carla Merling, who had put us in touch, and with the Hammers in Regensburg, who had taken care of the manuscripts during the war and later carried them across the border.

It was with indescribable joy that Hella Popp and I met again, re-united after I had placed a notice in the paper looking for her. Neither of us had known whether the other had survived the war. Her life had not been happy. Retired from teaching and married for the third time, she lived in picturesque Landsberg but was, unfortunately, plagued by vari-ous debilitating ailments. Elvins and I shall never forget the joy and en-thusiasm with which this most loyal and devoted of friends greeted me and continued to welcome us subsequently whenever we visited. She is dead now.

Emma also died a few years ago, but her daughter Susanna Feiertag-Erner has since been here for a second visit. She lives in Vienna, and we continue to be in touch with her and her son Sascha.

I have not attempted to find Erna Menta.

Nothing much has happened with the manuscripts since the 1987 con-cert. The hoped-for PH D thesis on Hans Feiertag and his music has not materialized, and the anticipated revival has not taken place. Not yet. But the manuscripts are safely housed in the Mahler-Rosé room in the University of Western Ontario's Music Library, and they are available.

Appendix

Appendix
Family and Friends

THE FAMILY

The family relationships mentioned in the journal are not as complicated as may appear. Simply put, my father Adolf Fischl had two brothers and my mother Ella Heitler had two sisters. The five families are as follows:

Karl (Charles) and Elisabeth (Lise, née Roth) Fischl (my father's older brother and wife), daughter Lilly and son-in-law Felix Munk (later anglicized to Monk)

Louis and Maña (née Steiner) Fischl (my father's younger brother and wife), daughter Lea and son John

Adolf (Ada) and Eliška (Ella, née Heitler) Fischl (my parents), daughters Hanna (Hanne, Hanni) and Annemarie (Mimi)

Anna (Antschi, née Heitler) and Otto Pollak (my mother's younger sister and husband), sons Hans (John) and Fritz (Friedl, Fred), and daughter Gerta (Gerti, Gertsch)

Milada (Milly, née Heitler) Samel (my mother's widowed sister), daughters Margit and Ruth. (Ruth remained in England.)

THE NEXT GENERATION

Below is further information for those wishing to know more about the Fischl-Heitler family, some of the New Canadians of 1939.

John Pollak My cousin John (son of Aunt Antschi) graduated in medicine from Queen's University and served in the Royal Canadian Army Medical

Corps. When the fighting ended, he returned to Czechoslovakia to marry his childhood sweetheart Zdĕna. He then spent a lifetime practising medicine, first in Burford, Ont., and then in Vancouver.

Fred Pollak, John's younger brother, also enlisted in the Canadian army and served in the Special Wireless Intelligence Unit. After the war, he chose to remain in uniform and rose to the rank of major. He married Ann Guthrie, daughter of Air Vice Marshal Guthrie.

Gerta Pollak Maclean is divorced and lives in Vancouver.

Margit Samel (Aunt Milly's daughter) was a student of applied physics at the University of Toronto when she met and married Lloyd Smith, a fellow student.

Lilly Fischl Monk   My cousin Lilly (daughter of Charles Fischl) and her husband Felix Monk joined Uncle Louis as partners in his glove-making business. Later they moved to Montreal and established their own firm, Paris Gloves. After their death, the business passed to their son, Peter Monk.

Lea Fischl McQuitty (daughter of Louis Fischl) and her husband Douglas McQuitty remained in Prescott. After a long struggle with cancer, Lea died in 1993.

John Fischl (son of Louis Fischl) and his wife Lise (née Belanger) live in Maitland, Ont.

Annemarie Fischl Rosenbluth   My sister Mimi had a successful career as a psychiatric social worker. She and her economist husband Professor Gideon Rosenbluth live in Vancouver.

Hanna Fischl Spencer and husband Elvins Spencer   I have followed Elvins to Windsor, Ont., Trail, B.C., Hull, Que., Saskatoon, Sask., and finally London, Ont., while he pursued his career as a research chemist, teacher, and administrator. Meanwhile, my experience was also broadened and varied. After working on gloves in Prescott and teaching at Elmwood, I was employed for a time as a social worker in Windsor and later got seriously involved with the Council of Women in Saskatoon and London. Along the way, I received a crash course in Canadian sociopolitical history, having married into a family that had an active part in helping shape it (see p. 189, n. 30). Finally, in 1959, I was able to return to teaching and became a member of the German Department at the University of Western Ontario, retiring as full professor.

FRIENDS

Finally, here are some details about the later lives of a few of the friends mentioned in the journal.

Joseph and Olga Auerbach and their children emigrated to Brazil, and we corresponded for some time afterwards. Unfortunately, we eventually lost touch. My search a few years ago, in particular for their children Daža, Helga, and Norbert, proved in vain.

Hella Popp   The joyous reunion with Hella has already been mentioned. It had been forty years since we last saw each other and we were jubilant that the other had survived. But the tables had turned, and now it was she who needed to be comforted: she was disillusioned and unwell. She had suffered through two unhappy marriages and was troubled because one of her daughters was handicapped. We later visited her and her supportive, patient third husband several times. Six years ago, an ominous black-edged note arrived informing me that she had died.

Hilda Cunnington, whose letter to Mr Blair saved my parents' lives, remained a lifelong friend. Hilda died in 1984, not long after visiting us in Canada. But fortunately, the Cunnington bond is holding and we have kept in touch with Michael and Nigel.

Susanna Feiertag Erner   Last but not least, Susi, daughter of Hans and Emma Feiertag, lives in Vienna and we keep in touch. At the time of writing her son Sascha is doing graduate work in physics at the University of Chicago.

Notes

INTRODUCTION

1 Now called Chomutov. Throughout the diary I have kept the place names we used at the time. See map, p. xviii.

2 Erich Heller later emigrated to England and America and became a prestigious writer and lecturer, a preeminent authority on German literary giants such as Goethe, Nietzsche, Thomas Mann, Rilke, and Kafka. The list of his publications, recorded in the *Festschrift* that was dedicated to him for his sixty-fifth birthday in 1976 – when he was Avalon Professor in the Humanities at Northwestern University, Evanston, Illinois – takes up seventeen pages.

3 For a detailed account, see Peter Gay, *My German Question: Growing Up in Nazi Berlin* (New Haven: Yale University Press, 1998); and Victor Klemperer, *I Will Bear Witness: A Diary of the Nazi Years 1933–1941*, trans. Martin Chalmer (New York: Random House, 1998).

4 Among the encouraging voices, those of Elizabeth and Bob Kymlicka were particularly persuasive.

CHAPTER ONE

1 My cousin John Fischl, son of Uncle Louis and Aunt Maña, with whom I was staying during the last few days of my summer vacation.

2 Even in this private diary I did not mention Hans's name, afraid that the journal might fall into the wrong hands. August 21 was his twenty-seventh

birthday; this is a coded hint that he hoped we might celebrate it together somewhere where nobody knew us. He had indeed just returned from a visit with his newlywed friends Hans and Marina Hammer in Berlin. I learned this in 1987 when Hans Hammer showed me their correspondence.

3 Bruno Brehm (1892–1974), Austrian novelist, popular in the 1930s. *Britta* (1934) was one of his minor works, about a wife and mother who deceives her workaholic scientist husband with his best friend.

4 Maña Fischl, wife of my father's younger brother. See appendix for details of family relationships.

5 A gallery in Prague that specialized in avant-garde art.

6 We passed each other without stopping to speak.

7 The Gymnasium (high school) where I had been reassigned to teach for a second year was in Olmütz (now Olomouc) in northern Moravia. In Czechoslovakia, the Department of Education made these decisions.

8 Growing up in the German-speaking part of the country – Komotau was entirely German – we called our parents "Mutti" and "Papa."

9 It goes without saying that "diary" stands for endearments that I did not dare write out, such as "Hansi" or "Hansl."

10 One step up from sessional, this would be the equivalent of a tenure-stream appointment in North America.

11 My younger sister Annemarie (see appendix), who in the meantime had also come to stay with Aunt Maña and Uncle Louis.

12 Walther von der Vogelweide (c. 1165–1230) is the most celebrated of medieval German lyric poets, the best known of the *Minnesinger*, the poets of courtly love. Walther broke with the traditional formula by writing charming lyrics that were simple, spontaneous, and seemingly came from the heart. His poems are filled with the love of life, a feeling for nature and the joys of love. I had come across his poems in my studies of Middle High German and had translated some of them into the modern idiom for Hans, who used them as the text when composing one of his major and most successful song cycles – his *Vogelweide Lieder*. For Hans and me, Walther was to have very special significance as an enduring bond and a symbol.

13 Franz Karl Ginzkey (1871–1963), Austrian novelist and poet. Several of his poems were set to music, and one of them became the anthem of Lower

Austria (Niederoesterreich). Perhaps the best known of his books is one written for children, *Hadschi Bradschi's Luftballon* (Hadschi Bradschi's Air Balloon), one of the most read children's books in Austria. First published in 1904, it has been republished many times (1904, 1933, 1943, 1960, 1968), each new edition altered and tamed to allow for modern sensibilities. Thus, Hadschi Bradschi, orginally a Turk, became a magician from the Orient, and cannibals were replaced by monkeys.

14 This was not, of course, a dream: even in my personal journal, I was afraid to reveal what actually happened.

15 Jonsdorf was, I believe, the name of this stop.

16 Priesen (now Březno) was a little town – really a glorified village – near Komotau, where we used to live, together with the Pollak family: my beloved Aunt Antschi, Uncle Otto, their daughter Gerta (Gerti), and sons Hans and Fritz (Friedl). Our two families were very close and visited often; Hans and Friedl lived with us while they attended high school in Komotau.

17 Erna Menta, a colleague and friend, and her student Helmar Frank; Frau Kassal was my landlady and Herta Weiss a student, all of them in Olmütz. Traudl Holub was my roommate during my final year as a student in Prague, after I left the Auerbachs (see below, p. 181, n. 39).

18 The agreed time when we would go to town to at least get a glimpse of each other "accidentally."

19 A former schoolmate.

20 Hella Popp, a friend from Prague days. We were in the same Germanistics program and both had Herbert Cysarz as thesis supervisor. Her home town Bärn is not far from Olmütz, and we were able to continue our friendship beyond university days. She proved to be the most – indeed, the only – loyal German friend.

21 Frau Mali Weisbach, a trusted friend of Hans in Komotau, many years older than us. She was one of the few who knew of our continuing contacts with each other and was willing to help us stay in touch.

22 Quarta: fourth year of the Gymnasium, roughly equivalent to grade 9. Our Gymnasium, still maintaining the way it was under the Austro-Hungarian monarchy, had eight grades, Prima to Octava. Students in Prima were ten years old (more or less), entering the Gymnasium after five years of elemen-

tary school and a qualifying exam. This was different from the way grades are counted in Germany; for some reason, their students start with the Sexta and advance up to the Prima.

23 We lived in Seegasse 5.

24 Pokorney Günther, the student from my Quarta.

25 The bumps: on birthdays and other celebratory occasions, your friends pick you up by your arms and legs and bump you up and down on the floor.

26 The Sudetendeutsche Partei (Sudeten German Party), led by Konrad Henlein.

27 All fellow teachers. It goes without saying that all members of the faculty were Germans. I was the only Jewish member of staff.

28 Another teacher.

29 *Klassenbuch*: the book in which school attendance was daily recorded; it also contained basic biographical information about the students.

30 Henleins: followers of Konrad Henlein; Nazis.

31 "Music Book for Maria Hav." Maria Hav, pronounced Haf, was the name Hans made up for me, creating a name out of my initials, which also were his: Hanna Fischl – Hans Feiertag. To be called Maria by the Catholic Hans was the ultimate compliment.

32 The last part of this little speech still rings in my ear. The translation defeated me, but for those who understand German, herewith what Lachnit said: "Man schaut sich einen Menschen doch an!"

33 September 1938 was indeed a fateful month for Czechoslovakia. The Henlein party had been getting ever more aggressive in its demands, and we frequently heard its members roar in unison, "Heim ins Reich!" and "Ein Volk, ein Reich, ein Führer!" ("Homeward into the Reich!" and "One Folk, one Country, one Leader!"). Contrary to what these slogans implied, the Sudeten region had never been part of Germany. Meanwhile, Hitler's speeches against Czechoslovakia, full of trumped-up charges, became increasingly more threatening, and a military attack seemed imminent. It was then that Britain and France, Czechoslovakia's allies (or so we thought), attempted to prevent war by sending Neville Chamberlain and Edouard Daladier to meet Hitler in Munich to negotiate a solution to the crisis – a crisis that had been deliberately concocted by Hitler and his Henlein followers. The Czechs were not invited to the table.

According to the agreement reached in Munich, Czechoslovakia was to cede the Sudetenland to Germany. In return, Hitler (who had annexed Austria a few months earlier) promised that this would be his last territorial demand. Chamberlain returned home, triumphantly declaring that he had secured "peace in our time."

But of course it was not to be. Encouraged by having been able to bully the Allies so successfully, Hilter was ready for further aggression. Only six months later, in March 1939, his army occupied what remained of Czechoslovakia – thereby, not coincidentally, achieving access to the flourishing Czech armament industry, which enabled him to invade Poland six months later and start World War II.

The Munich attempt at appeasing a dictator proved to be a mistake with catastrophic consequences, giving "appeasement" a bad name and making "Munich" eponymous with betrayal and week-kneed concessions to a tyrant.

34 Another challenge to the translator: "Colleague Suchanek" sounds odd, but we did address each other as "Herr Kollege" and "Frau Kollegin," and although in German this sounds less odd, it still sounds equally formal.

35 My landlady's family.

36 Milan Hodža, in his capacity as prime minister from 1935 to 1938, promoted cooperation with the Sudeten Germans.

37 Sokol: a Czech youth organization.

38 Ottla Kraus, my mother's cousin. Her husband, Uncle Max, was a diabetic.

39 While I was a student in Prague, I was employed by the Auerbach family as tutor and governess to their three children Daža, Norbert, and Helga. Josef Auerbach was a wealthy man who owned the Prague film studio on Barandov, which was tantamount to owning the Czech film industry. I lived with them for four years, treated as if I were a member of the family, in their fabulous villa on the brow of Barandov hill. The architect, Václav M. Havel, had evidently built the villa after Hollywood models. (It is his son who became president of the Czech Republic.) Josef and Olga Auerbach entertained frequently and lavishly, and there was never a dull moment in their household. To our mutual regret, I had to move out when I needed privacy and fewer distractions in order to finish my doctoral dissertation, but we stayed in touch and remained friends.

40 The young Jelinek cousins, Ada and Hanuš. Mimi is my sister, Antschi and Milly are my mother's sisters and Ruth is Milly's elder daughter (see appendix).

41 At this point in the original diary, I drew some ladybugs running across the page. For Hans and me (and possibly for others as well) ladybugs symbolized good luck and happy times.

42 Komotau, where I grew up, was predominantly German with just a sprinkling of Czechs – mostly railway workers and their families. In the main, the inhabitants were German nationalists who liked to boast, "Anderswo leben Menschen; in Komotau leben Deutsche" ("Elsewhere live people; in Komotau live Germans").

43 Mali Weisbach (see above, p. 179, n. 21).

44 Charles Fischl, my father's older brother. Klima was an official at the Ministry of Education.

45 Eduard Beneš, who had been president of Czechoslovakia since 1935.

46 A Henlein party functionary, friend of Bergmann. I never met him.

47 Erwin Guido Kolbenheyer (1878–1962), best known for his historic novels, such as *Amor Dei* (God's Love) about the philosopher Spinoza, and his three books about Paracelsus. He became very popular in the Hitler era. Simon Wiesenthal counts him among the apologists for the Nazis.

48 Hans and I, and our friend Mali Weisbach in Komotau, had agreed that in a pinch, when communication between us was impossible, she would serve as a go-between.

49 This is the first stanza, in modern German, of a well-known poem by Walther von der Vogelweide. It is one of the poems which I had transposed from the original Middle High German and which Hans set to music. It describes Walther sitting pensively on a stone, with legs crossed, elbow on knee, and chin in hand as he thinks long and hard how to survive in this world. The beauty and effect of the poem derives from the way in which Walther depicts his pensive pose, step by step, leading us to the central point of the piece: how to live in a world that is torn by strife.

50 It is interesting to note that some of the steadfast German nationalists had Czech names (Zapletal, Rozehnal, Suchanek). The symbiosis goes back a long way.

51 I still have it.

52 Yet another of the texts that I had drawn to Hans Feiertag's attention when
   I came upon it in my studies of German literature. He had made it into a
   song. Stefan George (1868–1933) was a somewhat austere, formal poet.
   What visual artists accomplished with brush and paint, he did with words.
   "Komm in den totgesagten Park und schau" is one of his more accessible
   and most beautiful poems, the first in the cycle *Das Jahr der Seele* (The Year
   of the Soul). Here the poet invites us, "Come into the park that has been declared dead, and look around," and he then proceeds to show us the many
   subtle hues and shades that are still there, weaving them into a a wreath.

53 I no longer remember who the author was.

54 A well-known tale from Czech mythology about a women's war.

CHAPTER TWO

1 Theodor Fontane (1819–98), prominent German novelist. This familiar re-
  frain from his novel *Effi Briest*, suggesting that there is no hard and fast
  answer, has been translated by D. Parmé as "It's a big subject."

2 Wehrmacht: German armed forces.

3 Rainer Maria Rilke (1875–1926) has been called one of the greatest lyric
  voices of the early twentieth century. *Das Stundenbuch* (Book of Hours)
  (1905) contains 133 poems, most of them addressed to a God who exists and
  evolves through art and the artist. Hans used several of these poems as texts
  for his songs and choral pieces. *Geschichten vom lieben Gott* (Stories of Our
  Dear Lord) are prose tales, the last of which (Told to the Dark) we found
  especially moving.

4 The infamous Kristallnacht was the night of 9–10 November 1938, when
  mobs throughout Germany and Austria vandalized Jewish stores, attacked
  and brutalized their owners at random, and destroyed synagogues and Jewish property. The devastation described by eyewitnesses, such as the histo-
  rian Peter Gay, is horrible beyond imagination. The fact that it happened
  simultaneously across the country left no doubt that it was ordered from
  above, unquestionably intended to dehumanize the Jews – who were already
  marginalized and crushed by countless humiliating edicts – in such a way

that they became outcasts, and contact with them became a taboo. See Peter Gay, *My German Question: Growing Up in Nazi Berlin* (New Haven: Yale University Press, 1998).

5 The Czech fascist party led by Rudolf Gajda.

6 Hella Popp, a friend from students days (see above, p. 179, n. 20). Gerta Kassal was my landlady.

7 Sylvia Segerfelt, a Swedish friend who had been a fellow student in Prague.

8 A Jewish student.

9 Makabi and Wizo: both are Jewish organizations.

10 Evidently a program of Feiertag music. Unfortunately, I did not dare mention the details in the diary. In retrospect, what a peculiar mixture these notes represent! Very frank in some ways but never mentioning his name. This paranoia about explicitly naming him – when anyone could so easily have found out – seems to have become a conditioned reflex.

11 My aunt Maña Fischl and friend Hella Popp.

12 A German member of the Czechoslovak parliament? Yes, the Sudeten Germans had their own representatives in parliament; they also had cultural autonomy, with German schools at all levels, including two universities, and German theatres, newspapers, etc., but that did not prevent Hitler and his puppet Konrad Henlein from claiming that the Sudeten Germans were an oppressed minority. With regard to the prediction that Hitler wanted to be in Prague by Christmas, Herr Kundt was out by a mere three months; but it is proof once again that the takeover of Czechoslovakia had already been decided, by Hitler and his Sudeten German followers.

13 Mrs Auerbach was my former employer (see above, p. 181, n. 39). Hans Pollak was my cousin.

14 See appendix for family members. Děda Steiner was Maña's father.

15 Maña's brother and sister-in-law.

16 Sylvia Segerfelt (see n. 7 above).

17 That was the year Hitler came to power.

18 Enclosed at this point in the diary are some tributes by former students.

19 In retrospect, as I write these notes sixty years later, it has occurred to me that I may have been to blame for her silence with regard to Hans. She may have actually given him my Kralupy address and when I denied having heard

from him, she may have felt that if he did not wish to be in touch, she should not intervene.

20 Of course I did not dare mail the manuscript directly to Hans. Hella was going to post it from Germany.

21 Gerta Pollak, my cousin.

22 When I wrote this sixty years ago, tongue in cheek, I thought the remark was supremely ironic. I could not have imagined that what seemed such an extreme idea would be surpassed by reality.

CHAPTER THREE

1 Reading these instructions now, a lifetime later, they don't seem at all outlandish. Used to the fussy central European cooking, I found these simple procedures and plain dishes – "naked as God created them," as Heinrich Heine said in similar circumstances – highly amusing.

2 Remembering how Mimi got out of Czechoslovakia still sends shivers down my spine. Like everyone else, she had applied at various places for an English work and entry permit, when she heard rumours of yet another committee (a group of Quakers in this case) that was said to be helpful. She presented herself, only to be told regretfully that their quota had been filled and that unfortunately this was the last one. Disappointed once again, Mimi was on her way out when they called her back: "Wait a minute … What did you say your name was? Annemarie Fischl? I believe we have your permit." Mimi knew it wasn't possible – this was, after all, the first time she had approached them. But, miraculously, it was true. It so happened that they had a spare spot within their last quota and, not wanting to waste it, had looked at applications received by another agency. It was Mimi's name and picture they had chosen to submit.

3 Ottla Kraus, my mother's cousin in Prague; mother of Hanuš (John) who was mentioned earlier. Ottla, her husband Max, and John were very generous to me when I was a student in Prague.

4 Later I learned that Mrs Marchington lost her job at the Andersons over this incident. I tried in vain to find her when we visited Sheffield after the war. Still later, when Hilda Cunnington visited us in London, Ontario, in

1984, I learned how our meeting had come about. Someone – was it Mrs Nichol or Mrs Marchington? – had called her to say that there was "a situation she would not like, involving a refugee." Hilda Cunnington had acted immediately.

5 The Charles Fischl family's hometown. Uncle Charles taught French at the Gymnasium. He had regularly taken students to Paris in summer, hence his connection with Paris.

6 Later, in Canada, Uncle Louis told me that it was really this letter that turned matters around. Mr Blair, the feared immigration tyrant, was so impressed by "my" elegant turn of phrase that he actually showed Louis the letter.

7 When we visited Hilda Cunnington in Sheffield in the 1980s, she took us to visit their former home. In contrast to the usual experience, it seemed even bigger than I remembered. It now houses the BBC. When the person who showed us round heard that Hilda had lived there, they interviewed her on her memories of the place. During bombing raids, all windows had been shattered, but otherwise it was not damaged. But it was sad to see the neglected garden. A bittersweet memory.

CHAPTER FOUR

1 The little lake in Komotau where we spent our summers, where I learned to swim, and where I first spoke to Hans Feiertag was the Alaunsee, so named because it was the site of a former alum mine.

2 My cousin, the daughter of Uncle Louis and Aunt Maña.

3 Lilly and Felix Munk. Lilly is my cousin, daughter of Charles and Lise Fischl.

4 Jacques (Děda) and Božena Steiner, Maña's parents. They never made it out. Although they had permits to come to Canada, they could not get exit visas and perished in the Holocaust.

5 For details of relatives, see appendix.

6 How were we able to buy a farm? After the Munich debacle when Britain and France gave in to Hitler's demands for the Sudeten, thereby dismembering Czechoslovakia, the British government tried to make amends by establishing a fund which was meant to help the truncated country recover. But when Hitler broke his promise that this was his last territorial demand and

marched into Prague, declaring the republic a German protectorate, the moneys that had been allotted to the recovery of Czechoslovakia were turned into a resettlement fund to assist Czech refugees. The fund was jointly administered by representatives from the British government and the Czech government in exile. When cousin John Pollak learned about this source of help, he applied for our families. Each of the three families (the Otto Pollaks, Adolf Fischls, and Milada Samel) received $200, in addition to their passage to Canada. With this $600 we were able to put down half the amount necessary to buy the house and 90-acre farm – worth $1,250 in 1939!

7 The eleven were my parents, my sister Mimi, and me; my mother's younger sister Antschi (Pollak), husband Otto, and children John, Fred, and Gerti; my mother's widowed sister Milly (Samel) and daughter Margit.

8 *koláče:* flat cakes made of yeast dough, topped with fruit or other fillings. A Czech specialty.

9 Maňa's brother Robert Steiner and wife Bertl were still in Czechoslovakia, unable to get exit visas. They did, however, survive the Holocaust.

10 This would have been Dr John Ralph, classics professor at the University of Western Ontario in London, Ontario.

11 Mimi and I, and cousins Gerti Pollak and Margit Samel.

12 CSR: Czechoslovak Republic.

13 Mythological founders of Prague.

14 Thomas G. Masaryk, principal founder and first president of Czechoslovakia, 1918–35.

15 SA: Sturm Abteilung (stormtroopers).

16 Sir Charles G.D. Roberts (1860–1943).

17 The opening of presents, literally "gift giving," which traditionally happens on Christmas Eve.

18 Translating *Klangbild* presents a challenge. Orchestral sound?

19 I did not know at the time that Anna Cooke (Mrs H.C. Cooke) was the honorary secretary of the Standing Committee on Refugees which Senator Cairine Wilson chaired, and was working closely with her.

20 Jenness was chief anthropologist at the National Museum.

21 Louis and Maňa Fischl.

22 Unfortunately, these children were not admitted after all. They presumably perished in the Holocaust.

23 As it turned out, they did not. After a ship with children aboard was torpedoed in the Atlantic, the Cunningtons decided that it was too risky. But their connection with the Crateaus continued and was to last a lifetime, with correspondence and visits in both directions.

24 Johann Wolfgang Goethe (1749–1832), Germany's preeminent poet, is a towering giant in world literature (a term, by the way, which he coined). With his great productivity, wide range of interests, extraordinary insights, and of course the quality of his work and world view, he left a legacy that cannot possibly be summed up in a brief note. His oeuvre and the secondary literature about Goethe take up library shelves that are measured in kilometres. Suffice to say that his most famous single work is *Faust*. In the eyes of modern readers, Goethe is above all a symbol, epitomizing the best in German culture and tradition. He represents humanity, wisdom, moderation, and open horizons. Reading Goethe in the Hitler era when I wrote my journal was a way of reminding ourselves that there was – or had been – an "other Germany."

The two works that we chose to read are rhapsodic poems about life's journey. "An Schwager Kronos" (loosely translated: To Brother Time) is a stirring ode to the driver of the stagecoach in which the young Goethe was travelling. The rocky journey, vividly captured in verse, is a metaphor for the journey through life. "Gesang der Geister über den Wassern" (Song of the Spirits above the Water) presents a river as a symbol of life. Man's career resembles the river, rushing headlong from its source in the mountain, then broadening and calming down.

25 Now the Apostolic Nunciature of the Vatican in Ottawa.

26 Only very recently did John Fischl (Uncle Louis' son) show me a letter from Mr Blair to his father, explaining that he had persuaded Mrs Buck to revoke her offer to me and to postpone the appointment for a year. I don't know what had happened in the interval, but I assume that dear Uncle Louis somehow got Mr Blair to relent. I am amazed on two counts: first, Mr Blair's attention to detail and his concern with individual immigrants, for better or worse (Did he never delegate?); second, the weight he put on Louis Fischl's advice.

27 The future Senator Bowman-Bell.

28 Mr Bowman's secretary, who had often visited us at New Haven.

29 This turned out to be the last time I heard from anyone from "over there."

30 Henry Spencer, the father of Edith and her brother Elvins, was an MP from 1921 to 1935. As whip of the Progressive Party in 1926, when the Liberals had a minority government, he played a significant role in forcing Mackenzie King to introduce progressive legislation, including the Old Age Pensions Act. Later he was a member of the Ginger Group, which helped found the Co-operative Commonwealth Federation (CCF). Throughout, his wife Zella was a great driving force and active partner.